Bitcoin Explained for Beginners

The Only Guide You'll Need in 2021 to Understanding and Investing in Bitcoin! (includes Blockchain and Ethereum)

Thomas Mahoney

Currency Publishing

CONTENTS

Chapter 1: What is Bitcoin?

Broadly speaking, Bitcoin can be categorized as a "digital currency." In many ways, Bitcoin works like any other form of money, with the exception that there is no physical money and transactions occur entirely through the Internet. There are other kinds of digital currencies out there, but Bitcoin is the most well known, widely used, and valuable at this time.

As we begin to dive in, it will be helpful to think about Bitcoin in two ways: both as a currency and as a technology. We will get in to the revolutionary technology behind Bitcoin later in this book. For now, however, let's look at Bitcoin as a currency.

Bitcoin as Currency

When we begin to think about Bitcoin as a currency, or a digital asset, there are two big questions that most people ask right away:

- How is the value of Bitcoin determined?
- How is it actually used?

How is the Value of Bitcoin Determined?

To answer the first question, it is helpful to think about paper money, like US dollars. When push comes to shove, there is really not much physical difference between a one hundred dollar bill and a piece of paper. The reason a one hundred dollar bill is understood as something more than a piece of paper is because of a consensus amongst citizens to accept that particular piece of paper as having a designated value that can be traded for goods and services. There are a lot of factors behind the scenes that bring a society to this agreement, but in a nutshell: any currency has value because enough people agree that it does is.

The same principle holds true for Bitcoin. Bitcoin's value is contingent on the number of people who are willing to accept it as payment, a group that is growing in size almost daily. Obviously, if nobody was willing to accept Bitcoin as a form of currency, it would be an undesirable thing to possess, nobody would want it, and it would be worth nothing. We can see by looking at the price of Bitcoin, however, that people do use it and it does have value. The price of Bitcoin at any given time is, like other commodities, determined by the relationship between supply and demand. As the level of demand goes up, the price of Bitcoin also increases, and vice-versa.

In the upcoming chapters, we will explore some of the reasons for why an increasing number of people are choosing to accept Bitcoin as a viable, or even preferable, form of currency. Before we get into that, though, let's get an overview of how Bitcoin is used. What does a Bitcoin transaction look like?

How is Bitcoin Used?

Bitcoin can be used much like any traditional currency, such as US Dollars or Euros. You can use Bitcoin to send and receive payments, make purchases, or even put BTC into a "savings account" for the future. Bitcoin can also be treated like an investment, similar to how one might invest in a stock.

Have you ever used a credit card to make a purchase online, or transferred money electronically form one account to another? When it comes to using Bitcoin for transactions, the process feels very similar in practice. We can make purchases by transferring a certain amount of Bitcoin directly from one account to another, from the buyer to the seller.

You can currently buy a lot of things with Bitcoin, but not everything. In order to make a purchase with Bitcoin, you will have to find a vendor who is willing to accept it as a form of payment. Many big name companies already offer Bitcoin options, including Subway, Microsoft, OkCupid, Whole Foods, Etsy, and Overstock.com.

New vendors from a wide range of industries are adding options for Bitcoin payment all of the time. As more people begin to participate in the Bitcoin economy all over the world, vendors are responding to the increasing demand from customers to accept Bitcoin.

How is Bitcoin Different?

One of the major barriers to entry in terms of Bitcoin is that a lot of people struggle with the idea of a currency that is not physical. When we think of traditional currencies (called "fiat") like the US Dollar or the Euro, we often think of paper money. Many of us are used to thinking about money as cash- as a tangible thing that we carry around.

In reality, however, most people don't carry around sacks of cash. The bulk of our money is stored in banks. Why is this?

Paper money has been standard for some time, but it is ultimately not very practical. It can be lost, stolen, or damaged easily. On top of that, there is nothing that ties a particular piece of paper money to any one person.

If you have your entire life savings stuffed under your mattress and you get robbed, there is nothing in the money itself that will point back to you as the owner. Unless the police happen to bust the robber, there is a good chance the money is just lost forever. It is largely because of this vulnerability that we rely on banks to store the bulk of our money for us. Banks guarantee a level of security in exchange for fees and a certain degree of control over the money we keep in our bank accounts.

Historically, banks have existed as essentially the only option for people to keep currency in a secure, centralized location, backed up with a guarantee. But, are banks really the best solution to the problem of storing our money?

Depending on a variety of factors banks can regulate, limit, and control the access we have to our own money. For example, we may not be allowed to withdraw more than a certain amount at a given time. We might be charged high transaction fees to move money between our different accounts. If a bank is hacked, millions of accounts can be affected because everything is stored on in one centralized database. Ultimately, most of us end up storing our money in banks despite the various pitfalls because there is no better alternative. We have no choice but to trust these institutions or risk stuffing cash under the mattress.

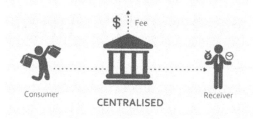

Bitcoin offers an alternative. Unlike traditional currencies, Bitcoin is decentralized. Transactions happen on a peer-to-peer basis without the need for a "middleman," like a bank, government agency, or other third-party institution. For this reason, Bitcoin and many other cryptocurrencies are often referred to as "trustless," meaning that we can make transactions without needing to put our trust into either the person we are transacting with or a financial institution.

If you're new to Bitcoin, you might be wondering how this works. In order to shed some light on the inner workings of this space, we need to switch gears for a minute and look at Bitcoin as a technology.

Wallet   Wallet

Consumer   Receiver

<u>Decentralised</u>

Chapter 2: Introduction to Blockchain Technology

One of the first terms you'll hear when delving into the world of cryptocurrencies is "blockchain." To understand Bitcoin, cryptocurrencies in general, and the future of decentralized computing, it is critical to understand the principles of blockchain technology. So, what is the blockchain and why is it important?

The blockchain is the framework, or "protocol," on which Bitcoin functions, as well as many other cryptocurrencies and emerging technologies. Essentially, a blockchain can be thought of as a public ledger that is distributed across many computers throughout the world. Each Bitcoin transaction that happens is recorded and added to the blockchain, as a new "block," and linked to the previous transaction with a special timestamp, like a link in a long "chain." The blockchain is managed through a distributed, peer-to-peer network, meaning that it is stored and updated continuously across many different computers all over the world. Anybody can run the software to turn their computer into a "node" in this giant network, helping to maintain this ongoing record of transactions. This distributed model means that a bunch of different copies of the blockchain exist all across the globe, which makes it essentially impossible for anyone to manipulate transaction information once it has been recorded.

Secure By Design

To help visualize the blockchain a bit more clearly, it is useful to imagine Fort Knox. Famously, Fort Knox houses the gold bullion depository for the United States. A boatload of gold is stored deep within Fort Knox. To keep this gold safe, Fort Knox employs armed guards, blast-proof vaults, and lots of other hardcore onsite security measures. If gold needs to be transferred, we can imagine armored vehicles and soldiers with machine guns keeping watch while the gold is moved. For a criminal to break into Fort Knox and steal the gold would be extremely difficult, not only because of the fortified compound, but also because gold, itself, is a heavy physical substance that would be difficult to move.

Banks (and many other institutions) have historically emulated a similar model when trying to protect assets, storing everything in centralized locations that rely on layers of security measures. Today, however, the vast majority of financial information exists digitally, in the form of data. We trust that banks have the cash to back up the numbers we see in our bank accounts, but for the majority of people at any given time those numbers are a record of value, rather than a physical cash amount stashed in a vault.

Rather than physical vaults, our financial assets exist primarily as financial data stored in the "digital vault" of a bank's server. Banks strive to make these servers into the digital equivalents of Fort Knox, but in reality this centralized model does not translate all that well into the modern landscape of digital transactions. Whereas it would require all kinds of dynamite, special equipment, escape vehicles, and Ocean's 11-style finesse to break into Fort Knox and steal gold, hackers are able to break into bank servers and steal financial information on a fairly regular basis using only computers. Credit card fraud, identity theft, and data breaches are all real threats that effect financial institutions almost daily.

Banks keep adding new layers of security around their "digital vaults" and hackers keep breaking into them. Fort Knox is fine for storing physical tons of gold, but this model begins to fall apart when we try to apply it to data in the digital realm. If we step back and look at the problem, we might begin to wonder if, instead of continuing to try to lock down one central server, there might be a better model for storing digital information and handling digital transactions. This is where the blockchain comes in.

Each block in the blockchain is linked to the previous block and recorded publicly across many different nodes all over the world. Rather than breaking into one central server and stealing or manipulating data, in order for someone such as a hacker to alter the blockchain, they would have to change the information not only one block, but on the entire blockchain, simultaneously, across the majority of the computers that store it all across the globe.

Technically speaking, this would require such a massive amount of computing power that it would be effectively impossible to accomplish under current conditions. This lack of centralized data storage makes the blockchain system secure by design. If somebody does try to enter a false transaction, for example by sending themselves Bitcoins that don't exist, the many different computers that maintain the blockchain will see that the math does not add up. If the math doesn't add up, the transaction will be deemed invalid and rejected, so it will not be added into the record on the blockchain.

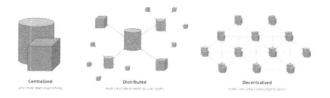

Centralized
what node does everything

Distributed
nodes distribute work to sub nodes

Decentralized
nodes are only connected to peers

Blockchain Technology Beyond Bitcoin

Blockchain technology is often associated exclusively with Bitcoin and other cryptocurrencies, but it also has much broader potential for a variety of applications, such as smart contracts, crowdfunding, governance, intellectual property, healthcare, file storage, the Internet of Things, and much more. Many industries are just beginning to explore the possibilities of distributed ledgers to manage resources and transactions. For this reason, blockchain technology alone is worth researching further for those interested in investment opportunities in emerging fields.

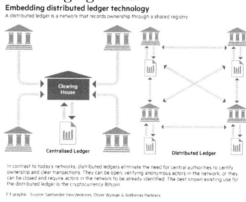

Embedding distributed ledger technology
A distributed ledger is a network that records ownership through a shared registry

Centralised Ledger

Distributed Ledger

In contrast to today's networks, distributed ledgers eliminate the need for central authorities to certify ownership and clear transactions. They can be open, verifying anonymous actors in the network, or they can be closed and require actors in the network to be already identified. The best known existing use for the distributed ledger is the cryptocurrency Bitcoin

FT graphic Source: Santander InnoVentures, Oliver Wyman & Anthemis Partners

How Do I Make a Bitcoin Transaction?

Let's look a bit more at how Bitcoin transactions work. You now know that records of all valid Bitcoin transactions are stored on the blockchain, but some readers might be thinking: Ok, cool, transactions are recorded on the blockchain... but what about my actual Bitcoins! Where are those stored and how do I actually make a transaction? Good question! The basic concepts of the blockchain are important in terms of understanding how and why Bitcoin works, but this doesn't really answer the question of how you actually add blocks to the chain.

Chapter 3: Bitcoin Wallets, Storage, and Transactions

Before you can actually get or spend Bitcoin, you need to have a place to put it. Bitcoins are stored in a digital Bitcoin address, which is called a "wallet." There are several different types of Bitcoin wallets, and we'll look at some of the most popular ones and go over how to create your own. Before we get into how to choose and create your wallet, let's look a bit more closely at how Bitcoin wallets work.

The crypto in the term "cryptocurrency" is a reference to cryptography, which is the study of secure communication. Contemporary cryptography relies heavily on complex mathematical algorithms that are deciphered by computers. To send messages containing sensitive information, people often encrypt their e-mails so that only the intended recipient will be able to decipher them. To a third party, encrypted e-mails will usually appear as complete nonsense, and unless they have the special password or key to decrypt the message, they will not be able to decipher the contents.

While modern encryption is almost always associated with digital information, cryptography has been around for centuries. Used predominantly be militaries, earlier forms of encryption included things like using secret codes to send messages through hostile territory. One of the most famous examples of Classical cryptography is the "Caesar Cypher," allegedly invented by Julius Caesar to communicate with his generals. The Caesar Cypher is a simple substitution cypher where certain letters in the original message are substituted with letters a specific number down from the original, creating a sort of "word scramble" that could only be understood if you knew the number of the shift and could then reverse the process to decipher the message.

Today, of course, encryption is typically a much more complex mathematical process. We all use different forms of encryption on a regular basis, whether we are conscious of it or not, such as an ATM pin number to access your bank account or the simple practice of using a password to unlock your phone. For sending sensitive information, many people use more complex systems with multiple layers of heavy-duty encryption.

Bitcoin wallets are secured using a kind of asymmetric encryption, sometimes also called "public key cryptography." If you have used tools like PGP encryption for sending email, this might sound familiar. If not, don't worry! Once again some wild math stuff happens in background, but actually using most wallets is very straightforward. There are two important parts to all standard Bitcoin wallets: a public key and a private key. These two keys are generated by an algorithm and usually just look like long strings of random letters and numbers.

The Public Key

The public key is the address for your Bitcoin wallet. This is a unique digital address, sort of like your "email address for Bitcoin." Everybody can see your public key. People will use this address, your public key, to send Bitcoin to you. Your public key address will also be recorded on the blockchain when you make a transaction, as Bitcoins either move into your wallet from somewhere else or you send Bitcoins from your wallet to another wallet's address (i.e. someone else's public key). Depending on how your Bitcoin wallet is set up, it is possible that your public key will be linked to your identity, either directly or indirectly. In fact, unless you are very intentional about taking advanced security measures to ensure your privacy, you should assume that it is possible for someone to link your public key address to your identity.

The Private Key

If your public key is like your "email address" for Bitcoin, the private key is like your password. Your private key is for your eyes only, and this is what allows you to access the contents of your wallet and send Bitcoins to other people.

When you send Bitcoin to someone else, it is the combination of their public key and your private key that makes the transaction valid. Your private key tells the system "Hey, I am really the owner of this wallet," and the public key tells it "this other wallet is where the Bitcoins should go."

Your private key is extremely important! If anyone else gets access to your private key, such as a hacker, they will be able to control your funds. There is pretty much no recourse if this happens, which is why it is vital to keep your private key secure. Unlike an email password, you can't simply "reset" your private key if you misplace it, so be careful. If you lose your private key, there is essentially no way to recover it and you will not be able to access your bitcoins!

Just as there are many different email providers available, there are also a number of options for creating a Bitcoin wallet. We will look at some of the most popular ways to create a wallet for Bitcoin, with the pros and cons of each.

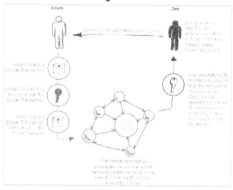

Source: https://tat.capital/bitcoin-and-blockchain-explained/

Chapter 4: Creating A Bitcoin Wallet

Before we dive into some of the different types of Bitcoin wallets, it is important to note that Bitcoin transactions are irreversible! If you are just getting started with Bitcoin, you will want to be sure to have a solid understanding of how your wallet works before making any major transactions.

Some wallets are more complex but offer greater levels of security and anonymity. Others are a bit easier but come with more reliance on a third party, such as a Bitcoin exchange. There are many different opinions throughout the Bitcoin community concerning best practices when it comes to wallets, and this space changes frequently as new options enter the market. Some people create a new wallet address for every single transaction and keep their Bitcoins spread out across multiple wallets. Some people keep all of their Bitcoins in one wallet and use that forever.

You can visit https://bitcoin.org/en/choose-your-wallet to see some of the many options available for creating a wallet, including mobile, desktop, hardware, and online wallets. Whatever form of wallet you end up using, it is important to remember that Bitcoin is real money and can be lost or stolen. We will cover the basics here, but if you plan to deal with large sums it is a good idea to become familiar with some more advanced security measures to protect your digital assets.

Online Wallets

Online wallets are one of the most abundant forms of Bitcoin wallet. Several online services, such as Bitcoin exchanges, offer the ability to store your funds online through one of their wallets. These wallets are easy to create, but generally anything that keeps your assets online is considered to be less secure. In fact, several of these services have been hacked or suffered from major security breaches in the past.

Obviously, anything that is connected to the Internet is more vulnerable to hacking or malware than something that is not on the Internet. Bitcoin wallets are no exception. Many people choose to keep the bulk of their Bitcoin offline and also maintain an online wallet with a small amount of funds for quick and easy online transactions.

Desktop / Mobile Wallets

There are several options out there to create Bitcoin wallets that can be stored on your computer and/or mobile phone. To an extent, these can offer more security than online storage through a third-party service. Once again, however, any device that is connected to the Internet is potentially vulnerable to malware. Unless you have a computer that you never connect to the Internet (this is called "air-gapped"), you can still be susceptible to cyber attacks.

Many wallets come with additional layers of encryption, password protection, and other security features built in, which can drastically reduce the risks. You will also have the option to create backups and add additional layers of encryption, which is a good idea. Generally, however, if you are dealing with a significant amount of Bitcoin, the safest way to store them is offline.

"Cold Storage"

Keeping your Bitcoin wallet offline, in a secure location, is generally considered to be the most secure way to store Bitcoin. It is common practice for people to keep the bulk of their Bitcoin offline, which is commonly called "cold storage," and only keep small amounts online for regular transactions. The downside to creating and using a cold storage wallet is that to do it effectively can be somewhat technically advanced. Services like BitKey, Armory, and others provide assistance in creating secure offline wallets.

Hardware Wallets

Hardware wallets are a popular combination of security and efficiency. Like the name implies, these are physical devices, similar in appearance to a USB drive or keychain that are created with the sole purpose of storing Bitcoin. In fact, many hardware wallets use USB to connect to a computer for making transactions. Even when connected to a compromised computer, good hardware wallets are immune to the kind of malware and viruses that can affect software wallets. Security, ease of use, and recovery options vary between models, so it is wise to spend some time reading reviews and comparing the features of different devices.

Choosing the Best Wallet

We've touched on some of the most popular options, but there are other methods of wallet creation out there. Security, complexity, and other features hold different priority levels for different people. Particularly for those who are planning to make a serious investment in Bitcoin, choosing a secure wallet option is highly recommended, even if it may require some additional legwork to set it up properly. Reading reviews, watching explainer videos, and asking around in Bitcoin forums, such as bitcointalk.org, are good ways to stay informed, ask questions, and choose the best wallet for your needs.

Follow this link to find a list of reputable wallets:
Bitcoin - Choose Your Wallet

Also be sure to download Cryptocurrency Secrets, the free book offered in this book which provides a more in depth analysis of your wallet options.

Chapter 5: How Do I Get Bitcoin?

Once you have somewhere to put your funds, you can actually get some Bitcoin! There are a number of ways that someone can get Bitcoin, but the most common are:

- By exchanging fiat currency for Bitcoin through an exchange

- Getting Bitcoin from someone else who already has Bitcoin

- Bitcoin mining

We will look at all of these methods, but before we dive in we should step back and look at a more fundamental question: Where do Bitcoins come from?

Where Do Bitcoins Come From?

Who "makes" bitcoins? This is an important question, and it is relates to another issue that you may be wondering about: how is the value of bitcoin determined?

To answer both of these questions, it is helpful to look briefly at where traditional fiat currency comes from. Broadly speaking, governments and institutions control the printing of paper money. The amount of money that is printed impacts the value of that currency in the global financial market. The economics behind how this all works can get pretty complicated, but in a nutshell: the more money a government prints, the less value that currency generally has. In economic terms, this principal is often referred to as "scarcity," meaning that the less there is of something and the more people that want it, the more value that thing has. This concept applies to commodities, fiat currencies, and Bitcoin.

There are many examples throughout history of situations where a government has printed tons of paper money to cover short-term expenses (almost always related to war), and as a result the value of that currency has plummeted. Probably the most well known example of this is the hyperinflation that occurred in Germany's Weimer Republic after World War I. People famously wallpapered their houses with paper money because it had so little value.

One significant way that Bitcoin is different than fiat currency is that there is a hard cap to the number of Bitcoins that will be created. No more than 21 million Bitcoins will ever exist. The last Bitcoin is estimated to appear some time around the year 2140. This built-in scarcity is one crucial aspect of how the value of Bitcoin is determined.

Still, however, we have not really answered the question of where Bitcoins actually come from. The short answer is that they are "mined" by Bitcoin miners.

Bitcoin Mining

If Bitcoins come from mining, it might be quite tempting to conclude that one should drop everything and become a Bitcoin miner. One of the first things that newcomers to the Bitcoin space often hear about is mining. At a glance, this can look like a primrose path to "free money." It can sound like mining is as easy as firing up an application your laptop and watching the Bitcoins come rolling in! Unfortunately, like most things involving "free money," the reality is that mining is not so simple.

Earlier we looked at the blockchain and how transactions are stored throughout a distributed network of computers. We know that each transaction is verified and added the blockchain, but how exactly does this happen?

This is where miners come in. Bitcoin miners use special software to solve complex math problems that are used to verify transactions, maintain the blockchain and add blocks.

By checking a new transaction against the public ledger of previous transactions (the blockchain), a "node" (a particular mining station) is able to distinguish between a valid transaction and an invalid one.

If someone attempts to spend Bitcoins that don't exist the system will say, "Hey, wait a minute, this doesn't match up with the history on the blockchain..." and the transaction will be rejected. Miners handle the heavy duty computer processing that it takes to check all new Bitcoin transactions, verify them, and add them to the blockchain.

In exchange for solving blocks, miners are rewarded with a certain amount of new Bitcoin, thus adding a little bit at a time to the global volume of available Bitcoins in circulation. This incentive encourages more people to mine, leading to a more secure system through wider distribution.

In the early days of Bitcoin, mining was something that could be done on pretty much any old computer and the reward for "discovering" a block was ample, while the overall value of Bitcoin was extremely low and there were not that many Bitcoins in circulation. Over time, as more and more people began to use Bitcoin, and also to become miners, the conditions changed.

Built in to the protocol behind Bitcoin is a relationship between the number of miners and the level of difficulty involved in solving the problem, or "mining" each block. In theory, we can imagine that if more miners enter into the scene, more blocks will be created at a faster pace. The Bitcoin protocol works in such a way that as more blocks are created, the rate of difficulty involved in solving the complex math problems required to successfully "mine" a block goes up. By making it harder to mine a block, the rate of block creation goes down. This relationship between the amount of Bitcoins that exist and the level of difficulty involved in mining new ones keeps the ecosystem stable over time.

The level of difficulty, today, required to mine a block is so resource-heavy, both in computer power and electricity, that it requires special equipment. In most cases, the cost of a mining operation far outweighs what one could hope to earn from mining Bitcoin for a very long time. Many miners today operate in collectives known as "pools," where members combine resources and split rewards. Joining a mining pool is one way to increase the odds of recouping the costs of mining equipment and potentially making a profit. It is still possible to earn Bitcoin today through mining, but it is definitely not easy or free to get started.

Buying Bitcoin

While there is still opportunity in mining, it is definitely not the most straightforward way to get your hands on some Bitcoin. It is much faster and easier to get existing Bitcoin from somewhere else, rather than trying to mine new Bitcoin.

When it comes to acquiring Bitcoin in this way, you have several options. No matter which route you take, you will need to set up a Bitcoin wallet to receive and store your funds.

Bitcoin Exchanges

In many countries, the easiest way to buy Bitcoin with fiat currency is through an online exchange. Bitcoin exchanges work essentially just like any other currency exchange, where you use one currency to buy another. At the time of this writing, Coinbase is one of the most popular (coinbase.com) Bitcoin exchanges in the US. Coinbase is an online platform that creates a Bitcoin wallet for you, lets you connect your bank account, and buy or sell Bitcoin through a very simple user interface.

Most Bitcoin exchanges involve transaction fees, and Coinbase is no exception. While it is technically "free" to use most Bitcoin exchanges, there will percentage fees associated with most or all transactions. It also not uncommon to experience delays when transacting through exchanges, which can range from mildly inconvenient to debilitating. Becoming familiar with the process and factoring fees and delay times into your transactions will make things run much more smoothly.

Most exchanges that allow you to buy Bitcoin with fiat currency will require you to link to a bank account and enter some personal information. This allows for fast, convenient movement between fiat currency and Bitcoin. Once again, it will be worth it to do some research and be sure to use an exchange that can demonstrate some longevity and has a good reputation.

Even then, it is generally not a good idea to store all or most of your Bitcoin in an online exchange. Mt. Gox, famously, was the world's dominant Bitcoin exchange for several years. At the height of its popularity, Mt. Gox handled around 70% of the world's total Bitcoin transactions. Then, in 2014, there was a massive security breach and approximately 850,000 Bitcoins were lost or stolen under somewhat mysterious circumstances. Exchanges are useful for moving funds between Bitcoin and fiat, trading, and actively transacting with Bitcoin, but the Mt. Gox fiasco is a good example of why it is not the best idea to keep all of your assets stored in an online exchange.

Bitcoin ATMS

Another way to buy Bitcoin that is becoming increasingly popular is through Bitcoin ATMs. These devices are cropping up all over the place, from malls to airports to city centers. They look a lot like traditional ATM's, but there are some important differences. Primarily, Bitcoin ATM's don't connect to any banks. They are connected, through the Internet, only to the universe of the Bitcoin network. Many Bitcoin ATM's allow for bi-directional exchange, meaning that you can either insert cash to be converted to Bitcoin and transferred to a public key address, or you can have Bitcoins from your own account converted into cash and dispensed by the machine. Some only handle transfers one-way or the other.

ATM's can provide a more anonymous way to buy into Bitcoin without syncing your bank account to a platform like Coinbase. However, there may be high transaction fees and limits on how much you can deposit or withdraw depending on the machine. One way that you can search for Bitcoin ATM's in your area is by using the Coin ATM Radar website at https://coinatmradar.com/.

Getting Bitcoin From Someone Else

Since the very beginning of Bitcoin, one of the most common ways to get started the currency has been to find someone willing to gift or sell some to you. As Bitcoin is a digital asset, it should not be too surprising that much of the Bitcoin community exists online. Forums such as bitcointalk.org or Reddit's r/bitcoin are good places to engage with other Bitcoin users. Some Bitcoin enthusiasts are happy to donate a small amount to a newcomer to help them establish their first wallet. After all, the more people that use Bitcoin, the higher the demand, thus the more valuable it will become, at least in theory. Through that lens, it makes sense from a long-term financial perspective to help new users get started even if means spending a little of your own coin initially.

There are also a variety tools online to find local Bitcoin exchanges, where people actually meet up offline, in person, to trade with Bitcoin. This can be a great way to avoid transaction fees, meet fellow Bitcoin enthusiasts in your area, and potentially increase the level of transaction anonymity. As with any scenario that involves meeting someone "from the Internet," use your judgment if meeting up to exchange Bitcoin locally.

Chapter 6: History of Bitcoin

We can nitpick about the precise moment in time that Bitcoin entered the mainstream. Generally speaking, however, even though there have been spikes in Bitcoin's value before, most would agree that 2016 – 2017 have marked a significant uptick in mainstream interest and adoption of both Bitcoin and blockchain technology. As a potential investor, it is useful to look at the history of Bitcoin to gain some perspective on how it has evolved. Studying the events and behavior that have shaped the current market can help us shape our vision of what the future may hold and make informed decisions.

Perhaps one of the most anecdotally interesting aspects of Bitcoin is the mysterious identity of its creator. Bitcoin first appeared in 2008 when a paper illustrating the concept was published to an email list for cryptography enthusiasts. The paper, written by a figure known as Satoshi Nakamoto, was called, "Bitcoin: A Peer-to-Peer Electronic Cash System."

A few months later, in January of 2009, Satoshi Nakamoto implemented Bitcoin and released the code as "open-source" (meaning that anyone can look at the code). Nakamoto mined the first block of Bitcoins, sometimes called the "genesis block," which started the bitcoin blockchain.

Although a few people have claimed either to be Nakamoto or to know his/her/their true identity, none of these claims have ever borne out. To this day, the identity of Satoshi Nakamoto remains a mystery. Nobody knows if Satoshi is one person, a group of people, a secret society, or the alias of a nation state actor. What is known is that he/she/they are thought to have mined around a million Bitcoins in the early days of the blockchain. At that time, of course, Bitcoin had a tiny user base and little value as a currency.

One of the most famous early Bitcoin transactions was the exchange of 10,000 BTC for a delivery of two pizzas. Today, of course, 10,000 BTC would be worth upwards of $20,000,000! At the time, Bitcoin was mostly seen as a subcultural novelty that a small group of people were beginning to experiment with.

Many people hear about the drastic increase in Bitcoin's value over the past few years and wonder if it is too late for them to make money by investing in Bitcoin. Of course, everybody wishes that they had bought Bitcoin earlier, but speculation still plays a huge role in the Bitcoin community.

Will the price of Bitcoin skyrocket again, will it rise slowly over time, or have we seen the height of its value already? These are the kinds of questions that draw many people to Bitcoin today.

Chapter 7: Making Money With Bitcoin

Investing in Bitcoin

Particularly as Bitcoin has become more popular, there is a lot of advice floating around on how to make money with Bitcoin and other cryptocurrencies. In reality, there is no secret, easy foolproof method to invest $100 and come out with $10,000. As with any market, Bitcoin trading is a system of risk and reward and there are no guarantees. Just because Bitcoin is a digital currency does not mean you can't lose "real money." Of course, you can make real money, too, but it is important to remember that this is a high-risk space.

Compared to traditional markets, the cryptocurrency space is extremely volatile. Prices can fluctuate significantly over one day, or even one hour. It is not uncommon to see values swing up or down by 20% or more in 24 hours. Particularly for traders coming from traditional markets, the peaks and crashes in the cryptocurrency space can certainly get your adrenalin pumping.

Many people have made the mistake of hearing about Bitcoin (or another cryptocurrency) for the first time, usually as a result of some hype, and immediately buying in while the price is at a high, thinking they will get in before it goes up even more. Then they see the price of the currency plummet. In a panic, they sell it all off to cut their losses before it sinks any more, only to see it level out or soar again a few days (or hours) later. There is no way to guarantee that this will not happen even to savvy traders, but you can do a lot to improve your odds of success.

The single most important thing you can do as an investor in the cryptocurrency world is to do your own research. Arm yourself with good resources and take the time to study the trends. Particularly as Bitcoin has entered the mainstream, there has been a huge rise in self-proclaimed Bitcoin gurus, some of whom are more credible than others. Explore freely, but keep in mind that anything promising "instant wealth" is worthy of healthy skepticism.

A great way to get familiar with the landscape of Bitcoin exchanges is to spend some time looking at the charts. Study the peaks and dips, level of stability, and researching any anomalies. Did something happen at a certain point to trigger a huge jump or drop? Was there a significant global event, did an article come out in a popular magazine, did an industry leader begin accepting Bitcoin? Could a similar thing happen again? These are good questions to consider. Almost all Bitcoin exchanges have charts that graph the historical trends and offer real-time updates on value, volume, and other statistics. Coinmarketcap.com is one popular website that offers daily overviews, history, and information on a wide variety of cryptocurrencies.

The more information you have, the better equipped you will be to see new opportunities and avoid common mistakes. Get to know the Bitcoin space, read articles, engage with the community, and explore the tools and resources available. Nobody can predict the future, but the more aware you are of trends on a moment-to-moment basis, the more likely you are to anticipate the behavior of the markets correctly. What you ultimately choose to do with your money is your business, but one famous adage that you may want to keep in mind is: "Don't invest more than you can afford to lose."

Bitcoin Exchanges & Trading

When it comes to "trading with Bitcoin," there are several ways that this can happen. The most basic way to do it is to buy Bitcoin with fiat (US dollars, Euros, etc.), wait for the price of Bitcoin to go up, and then exchange it back into fiat. Of course, there is no guarantee that the price will go up; it could just as easily go down. Being familiar with the trends, history, and current affairs can help you make informed decisions about when to buy in and cash out.

Some firm believers in Bitcoin might argue that this approach of trading between Bitcoin and fiat "misses the point." On an ideological level, there are valid reasons for that sentiment. Realistically, however, many people see Bitcoin as an investment and not a "replacement" for fiat currency. Whatever your opinion on the matter, the fact remains that people have increased their wealth by using this approach.

You can find a list of online exchanges that deal with trading between Bitcoin and national fiat currencies at https://bitcoin.org. To do this type of trading successfully, you will also want to be very conscious of transaction fees, delay times, and exchange reputability. These factors can all differ between exchange platforms and can change in response to any number of events or circumstances. All exchanges come with their own unique pros and cons.

Accessibility to certain exchanges may depend on your nation of residence.

Some of the most popular exchanges in the US are Poloniex, Bittrex, GDAX, Coinbase, and Kraken. Once again, all of these have different features and may be more suited to a particular set of needs. Coinbase is widely considered to be one of the easiest platforms for beginners, as it allows you to buy Bitcoin with a large variety of national fiat currencies through a very user-friendly interface.

Bitcoin exchanges, in general, have an initial learning curve for many people, particularly those who are new to markets and trading. Even those coming from a background in the stock market may find that Bitcoin exchanges take some getting used to. All exchanges tend to have different rules, spending limits, levels of verification, security practices, and tools available. Plus, not all exchanges deal in all cryptocurrencies. Generally, however, all exchanges do trade primarily in Bitcoin.

"The Fast Nickel or The Slow Dime"

There is an expression that you may have heard before in relation to investing: the fast nickel or the slow dime. Essentially, this means making a little bit of profit in the short term or a larger profit over the long term. When it comes to trading Bitcoin, there are plenty of people who employ both of these strategies.

Some investors choose to buy Bitcoin once, ideally when it the value is low, and hold on to it, believing that the price will trend upwards over time and eventually pay off big-time. Obviously, this worked out very well for early adopters who held on to their initial Bitcoin investments. Some speculate that Bitcoin will undergo another massive price increase in the future. These folks will continue to hold tight to their Bitcoin throughout price fluctuations, hedging their bets on long-term growth. This would be the "slow dime" approach.

(Buying into a cryptocurrency and holding on to it is often called/spelled "hodling" in online cryptocurrency communities).

There are others who watch the space diligently and regularly shift funds back and forth between Bitcoin, fiat, and other cryptocurrencies, taking advantage of minor price fluctuations, somewhat similar to Wall Street-style day trading. These speculators aim to buy when prices are low and sell when they go up to make a quick profit (the "fast nickel"). Often the gains are smaller using this approach, but enough successful trades can add up quickly.

While trading between fiat and Bitcoin is one way that people can make (or lose) money, trades in the cryptocurrency space often involve exchanging one cryptocurrency for another, rather than trading with fiat. Bitcoin is, in this context, sort of like the "gateway" cryptocurrency.

Trading Between Cryptocurrencies

There are hundreds of crytocurrencies out there besides Bitcoin, with varying levels of value, volume, and potential. An active trading culture exists surrounding a number of these alternative currencies (often called "alt-coins"). Some examples of popular alt-coins include Ethereum, Litecoin, and Dogecoin. In order to buy into to most alt-coins, one usually needs to have Bitcoin to begin with. Most alt-coins cannot be purchased directly with fiat, but rather with Bitcoin, although there are some exceptions.

The alt-coin space is a bit of a "wild west," where high risks can lead to high rewards or big losses. Remember the early Bitcoin adopter who bought 2 pizzas? For many, the appeal of investing in alt-coins is that they have the potential to increase dramatically in value, like Bitcoin did. If an alt-coin is backed by a promising application and strong development team speculators may invest if they see potential for growth. Hedge funds have even begun to emerge dealing exclusively in cryptocurrencies and blockchain technology.

The emerging paradigm of blockchain-based currencies and applications has led to a huge surge of speculative investment in this space, which in turn has led to an abundance of new "alt-coins" competing to lead the way in different specialized use cases. Ethereum, for example, is widely seen as second to Bitcoin as the most popular cryptocurrency. There are some who believe that Ethereum will surpass Bitcoin in both value and popularity, and have hedged their "slow dime" bets by investing in Ethereum. Likewise, there are many who have invested in other promising newcomers to the space and are willing to wait five years or more for the value to increase.

For serious investors interested in emerging technologies, the cryptocurrency and blockchain space beyond Bitcoin is extremely promising. Like many up-and-coming tech spaces, there is also a lot of noise to sift through. Everybody has an opinion on the future of blockchain technology, and obviously they can't all be correct. Listening to others is a great way to learn, but it is up to you to form your own opinions and decide what's in your best interest.

Getting Paid in Bitcoin

Bitcoin's value and long-term viability is largely dependent on how many people are willing to accept it as a form of payment. With the recent rise in mainstream recognition, more and more vendors are offering the option pay for goods and services with Bitcoin.

Historically, the volatility of Bitcoin has made many businesses reluctant to adopt it as a payment option. Today, however, more and more companies are integrating options for Bitcoin payment into their business model. You can now pay for things like plane tickets, online classes, cheeseburgers, and much more with a Bitcoin transaction.

For freelancers, small businesses and entrepreneurs, getting paid in Bitcoin is one way to invest in the currency. If you get paid in Bitcoin for a service and the value of Bitcoin goes up more than the value of whatever fiat currency you would have otherwise been paid in, you can continue to earn even after the job is over. Of course, it bears repeating that the opposite could happen, as well. Many people set up wallets to accept tips in Bitcoin, which can be a fun way to get your feet wet without staking too much.

Bitcoin Faucets

If you spend some time online searching Bitcoin topics, you will likely come across a mention of Bitcoin "faucets." These are websites that you can visit to receive very small amounts of Bitcoin for free every so often. Most faucets operate by giving away a "trickle" of free Bitcoin, while actually making money by showing ads on the webpage. Some faucets feature games, such as digital dice, which yield higher or lower rewards from the faucet. Generally speaking, you will not make very much money from faucets, although if you make a point of visiting every day over a long period of time it can add up.

Chapter 8: Common Myths, Mistakes, & Misconceptions About Bitcoin

If you've been reading along, you should feel pretty confident that, at this point, you have a handle on the basics of Bitcoin and blockchain technology. You have the tools in your toolkit to set up a Bitcoin wallet, get yourself some Bitcoin, and make transactions. That being said, in order to really hit the ground running there are a few common misconceptions about Bitcoin that are worth covering in order to avoid falling into traps, making mistakes, or getting swindled.

Anonymity: Is Bitcoin Anonymous?

Something that is often mentioned in articles about Bitcoin is that it is "anonymous." This has created a lot of confusion, but ultimately the short answer is: No, Bitcoin is not anonymous!

We know that Bitcoin transactions are recorded on the blockchain as transfers from one public Bitcoin address to another. There are ways to increase the level of privacy surrounding transactions, but anonymity is not necessarily achieved by default when looked at in context.

For example, when you buy Bitcoin with fiat currency from an exchange that is linked to your bank account, such as Coinbase, your funds are deposited into a particular Bitcoin wallet address. In this scenario, there is a clear link between your bank account to your Bitcoin address.

Because every Bitcoin transaction is stored, forever, on the publicly accessible blockchain, anyone can observe the activity of a particular wallet's public address. In theory, it is possible to achieve anonymity by avoiding any behavior that might link a wallet's public address to that wallet's owner. In practice, however, when converting between Bitcoin and fiat, information about a user's identity often becomes public, or at least accessible to third parties. It is best to proceed with the assumption that Bitcoin is secure, but not anonymous by default.

Is Bitcoin Taxable?

Many people, often under the previous misconception that Bitcoin is "anonymous" or "untraceable," make the assumption that Bitcoin is not subject to taxes. This is wrong, at least in most countries.

In the US, the IRS treats Bitcoin and other forms of digital currency as an asset, like property, not as a currency. This means that you will be subject to capital gain or loss when dealing in digital currency. Additionally, if you are getting paid in Bitcoin, either as an individual or a business, your income is also subject to tax. According to the IRS, taxpayers must report transactions made in Bitcoin according to their value in US dollars.

An in-depth analysis of tax law in relation to Bitcoin is beyond the scope of this book, but for serious Bitcoin investors it is important to do your homework to avoid getting into trouble with the IRS. You can view the IRS Virtual Currency Guideline online at https://www.irs.gov/uac/newsroom/irs-virtual-currency-guidance

Is Bitcoin Used By Criminals

While popular media such as TV shows and movies have certainly played a role in introducing Bitcoin into the mainstream, it is almost always portrayed as being used for illicit transactions in some sort of criminal context. It has even been suggested that Bitcoin is used primarily by terrorists! While it is true that illegal goods and services are sold online, particularly on the "dark net," the reality is that the vast majority of Bitcoin users are not involved in criminal activity.

In large part due to the public ledger of transactions, and, once again the fact that Bitcoin is not anonymous by default, Bitcoin is not an ideal currency for conducting criminal transactions. To this point, the famous Winkelvoss Twins, founders of the popular Gemini Bitcoin exchange, have suggested that Bitcoin is only used by "stupid criminals."

The conflating of Bitcoin with shady dealings is due in no small part to the aforementioned incident with the popular Mt. Gox exchange. The dubious circumstances surrounding the loss of a huge number of Bitcoins from Mt. Gox led to a lot of reports that painted Bitcoin itself as the culprit, rather than the poor management of the Mt. Gox exchange. Similarly, when the famous "Silk Road" website, used largely for selling illegal drugs and other items through the dark web, was shut down by the FBI in 2013, many people conflated this incident with Bitcoin itself being "shut down."

Bitcoin can be difficult to understand, and it is easy to see how a lot of media coverage in the earlier days of Bitcoin failed to distinguish between Bitcoin itself and various platforms that were built on top of it, such as Silk Road and Mt. Gox. Today, public opinion is changing rapidly as Bitcoin is gaining traction all over the world, but there are still many people out there who are under the impression that there is something inherently illicit or illegal about Bitcoin.

Is Bitcoin a Ponzi Scheme?

"Ponzi Scheme" has become a buzzword in relation to many cryptocurrencies. There are definitely some "alt-coins" out there that might be Ponzi Schemes, but Bitcoin is not one of them.

Ponzi Schemes work by promising huge rewards to entice investors to put money into a concept that is never really actualized. Bitcoin's decentralized structure means that there is no CEO or "head of Bitcoin" to swindle investors. Furthermore, Bitcoin has never made any guarantees concerning market value. Anybody familiar with Bitcoin will tell you that it is extremely volatile and there is no knowing if it will go up or down on any given day. Finally, the defining characteristic of a Ponzi Scheme is that is offers no real value. We see new examples of real-world applications of Bitcoin and blockchain technology across a variety of industries on an almost daily basis, backed by a broad consensus within the tech community that this is a revolutionary technology that is not going to go away any time soon.

Chapter 9: The Future Of Bitcoin

The future of Bitcoin appears both unpredictable and unstoppable. Nobody knows exactly what will happen, but it certainly appears that Bitcoin has entered far enough into the mainstream that there is no going back. We have seen a wide variety of major industries including airlines, tech companies, security agencies, and the financial sector begin to open up to Bitcoin and, perhaps even more significantly, to the underlying blockchain technology. The growing demand for talented blockchain programmers across a broad spectrum of industries is evidence that the era of blockchain technology is upon us.

A new generation of entrepreneurs has just begun to emerge in the cryptocurrency and blockchain space, developing innovative applications around Bitcoin, both as a currency and a technology. Whether Bitcoin as a currency will continue to rise in value and dominate the cryptocurrency markets or whether it will be knocked from its position by a disruptive newcomer is something that only time will tell. Diversifying your cryptocurrency investments is seen by many as one way to increase your odds of picking a winner.

Hearing stories about early Bitcoin adopters who made millions can make some people who are just learning about Bitcoin feel as though they are too late to the game. Whether Bitcoin as a currency is the "one coin to rule them all" is unknowable, but the promise of blockchain technology is still just beginning to take hold in the mainstream, bubbling to the surface of a vast sea of opportunity. There is no crystal ball to show us precisely what the future looks like, but one thing is certain: this is just the beginning. Five or ten years from now, people who invest wisely today may very well be seen as "early adopters."

Blockchain

As cryptocurrencies like Bitcoin gain popularity around the world, a considerable uptick in attention from mainstream media outlets has brought the term "blockchain" out of obscurity and into the spotlight. "Blockchain" has even become a bit of a buzzword in the tech and financial sectors, and increasingly in other fields and industries.

There is a lot of hype surrounding the concept of the blockchain, but what does this term actually mean? What is blockchain technology? What does it do? How does it work? Why does it matter? These questions are not always answered with due diligence in the sea of headlines and "think pieces" that deal with digital currencies and other applications using blockchains. As a result, many people are left with an incomplete understanding of this transformative new technology and its implications for the future.

One challenge when learning about blockchains is that much of the real power behind the scenes of this technology involves complex mathematical processes that can be difficult to grasp for those of us who do not have advanced degrees in computer science or a background in cryptography. Unless you plan to become a developer and build your own blockchain applications, however, you can gain a thorough understanding of how blockchains work on a practical level without needing to tackle any algorithms.

The goal of this book is not to plumb the depths of the mathematical wizardry used to code blockchain-based applications, but rather to serve as an introduction to the broader architecture and conceptual background behind blockchain technology. We will take a practical approach, examining how blockchains are used in the real world, how they work, and why this technology is being hailed as revolutionary by many prominent voices around the world.

When the Internet arrived, it completely transformed the structure of daily life across the globe. Many people believe that the implications of blockchain technology will give rise to a paradigm shift of similar scale. Blockchain is a foundational technology that has the potential to reshape the nature of institutions, industries, and the global economy.

Before we set the world on fire, however, let's get back to the basics: what is a blockchain, how does it work, and what exactly does it do? These are some of the fundamental questions we will set out to answer throughout the course of this book. First, however, as we begin to explore this technology of the future, it is helpful to get an overview of its past. Where did the idea of blockchain come from?

Chapter 1: A Brief History of Blockchain Technology

The concept of a "blockchain" was introduced in 2008 by Satoshi Nakamoto as part of the protocol behind the digital currency Bitcoin. Nakamoto published a technical paper to an email list that was popular amongst cryptography enthusiasts that laid out the basic principles behind both Bitcoin, a digital currency, and the blockchain, the underlying technology behind that currency.

Shortly thereafter, in 2009, the first blockchain was put into implementation when the first Bitcoin was mined by Nakamoto and put into circulation. Today, Bitcoin has achieved global renown and is accepted as a valid currency by increasingly more vendors. You can buy everything from airline tickets to online courses using Bitcoin; even Burger King has started to accept it!

Over the past decade, many other digital currencies often called "cryptocurrencies," have emerged utilizing blockchain technology to manage transactions. We will look at some of these in subsequent chapters of this book, but it is important to keep in mind that the implications of blockchain technology reach far beyond the realm of digital currencies.

While cryptocurrencies, and specifically Bitcoin, were the first applications to use blockchains, many industries are beginning to explore blockchain tech as a way to handle a wide range of procedures, including smart contracts, data storage, and resource management. Throughout this book, we will look at several different ways that blockchain applications are being developed both pertaining to cryptocurrencies and in other fields.

Anecdotally, one of the more fascinating details in the history of blockchain technology is the identity of its creator. Although there are many theories, nobody has ever uncovered the true identity of Satoshi Nakamoto. Whether Nakamoto is an individual or a group of people, we may never know. What is certain, however, is that their contribution to the future of technology is incredibly significant. Many prominent thinkers and voices from within the tech industry see revolutionary potential for blockchain technology, and with good reason!

Chapter 2: Blockchain Basics - Managing Digital Transactions

There are several underlying concepts that make blockchain technology uniquely suited to handle digital transactions. Today, the most well-known and widely implemented application of blockchains is found in the cryptocurrency space, where blockchains are used to handle financial transactions that happen digitally on a peer-to-peer basis.

While the applications for blockchain technology are not limited exclusively to digital financial transactions, this is a good place to begin exploring how blockchains work in a real-world context. Digital currencies, pioneered by Bitcoin, have emerged as a new asset class, which is remarkable in and of itself. Beyond the emergence of digital assets, the blockchain framework also provides a model for rethinking institutional structures in terms of how power is organized and value is distributed. We are still in the early stages of exploring the possibilities for blockchain technology, but the space is developing quickly. It is not an understatement to suggest that blockchain technology will fundamentally reshape the nature of governments, personal property, and the global economy within the next decade.

In order to get a clearer picture of how blockchains work, it is helpful to begin by looking at digital currencies, like Bitcoin. Digital currencies are, as of now, the most well-established implementations of functioning blockchains. In the case of digital currencies, or "cryptocurrencies," blockchain technology is used to handle financial transactions. Before we look at how the blockchain model works, it is helpful to look at how financial transactions have worked historically.

How We Handle Financial Transactions

For centuries, people have relied on centralized institutions like banks and governments to serve as intermediaries when it comes to storing and transacting financial assets.

As a practical matter, most people keep the majority of their finances stored in a bank. There are many advantages to this. If for example, you had your entire life savings buried under the floorboards of your house and your house burned down, you would be in big trouble. Banks provide a promise of security, protecting your assets in exchange for various transaction fees. We trust banks to keep our funds secure in exchange for a percentage of our money. Over time, this model of keeping money in banks emerged as the norm. In an increasingly digital world, however, many people have begun to search for alternatives to the historical model of consolidating resources in centralized institutions.

Today, as more and more transactions take place digitally, the need for trust and security has become even more significant. Financial information exists largely as data, and transactions are ultimately just file transfers. Without a secure process, it is incredibly easy to manipulate data. Hackers regularly compromise bank servers, ATM machines, and other places where financial data is stored or transactions occur.

One of the biggest challenges of managing financial transactions on a peer-to-peer basis is the "double-spending problem," or how to ensure that someone isn't spending the same money twice. When Bitcoin arrived on the scene, it offered a solution to this problem, enabling direct peer-to-peer transactions to take place in a secure way that did not require trust from either party or a third-party intermediary, like a bank. That solution was the blockchain.

What is a Distributed Ledger?

While Bitcoin paved the way with blockchain technology, many subsequent applications, including but not limited to other digital currencies, have been built on the blockchain framework. One of the fundamental concepts driving the success of blockchain technology is its use of a distributed ledger system.

Ok, so what is a distributed ledger? Basically, a distributed ledger is exactly what it sounds like. A ledger is just list of records. Instead of keeping this list in one place, a distributed ledger is stored in many different locations simultaneously. Not all forms of distributed ledgers are blockchains, but all blockchains use some version of a distributed ledger.

Decentralization is one of the core concepts behind blockchain. By keeping multiple copies of the record of transactions in different locations all across the world, visible to anyone, the need for a "trusted" third party institution to serve as a middleman and oversee transactions is eliminated.

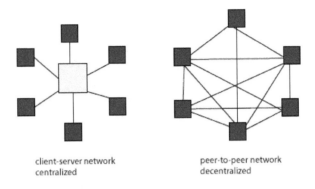

client-server network
centralized

peer-to-peer network
decentralized

To delve a bit deeper into how distributed ledgers work, let's imagine a hypothetical situation: pretend you have a big three-ring binder where you write down every financial transaction you make in a year. Anytime you make money or spend money, you write down the details in this binder. Only one binder exists and you keep it in your desk. A lot of things could go wrong in this scenario: your house could burn down, a nefarious person could sneak in and tamper with the information, you could forget to include a few documents and end up with numbers that don't add up, or any number of other unfortunate mishaps.

Instead of having only one binder, imagine that hundreds of thousands of identical copies of this same binder existed in desks of people all across the world. Every time any detail was added into the binder, the information would have to be checked against all of the copies to make sure that the numbers added up correctly, and the new information would be added into all of them at once. If once binder contained a transaction that didn't show up in any of the others, we could assume that binder was faulty. Now, in order for someone to tamper with your information, they would have to tamper with every single one of these binders all over the world at the same time.

Obviously, using a system of binders in desks is not very practical. In the virtual world, however, this is actually somewhat similar to how a distributed ledger works. In blockchains, each individual transaction, no matter how big or small, is recorded in a "block."

Each block contains a special timestamp that links it to the previous block. This allows computers to check each proposed transaction against the previous one. If the timestamps do not add up properly across the majority of computers, the transaction will be rejected. If the majority agrees that the proposed transaction is valid, it will be verified and added to a new block in the chain, or a new record in the ledger. Now, the next proposed transaction will be checked against that block's timestamp, and so forth.

In order for someone, such as a hacker, to enter false information into the blockchain, they would have to alter the information not only on one block but on every single block on the entire blockchain simultaneously across the majority of participating computers all over the world. Even with current technology, to accomplish that would require such a massive amount of computing power that it is effectively an impossible feat. Thus, the blockchains distributed ledger system is secure by design.

Because each transaction is checked against the entire history of previous transactions by multiple machines all distributed all over the world, it is impossible for someone to "cheat" the blockchain by attempting to spend the same money twice. One of the transactions will not match the historical record, and it will be rejected as invalid.

Not only is the "double spending" problem solved but transactions do not require either party to trust the other or a third party institution in order to be conducted. Person A cannot claim that they sent Person B money that "got lost in the mail" and Person B cannot claim that they "never received the money." All transactions are publicly visible, and therefore both parties will be able to see a record of the transaction on the blockchain.

Blockchain and Bitcoin

One of the most confusing and misunderstood aspects of the blockchain, as a concept, comes when we try to uncouple it from Bitcoin. As stated previously, Bitcoin is simply one application built on a blockchain framework. It is also the first, largest, and most well known functioning open blockchain in the world. Bitcoin's implementation of blockchain technology is often cited as definitive, meaning that when people say "blockchain" they are often talking specifically about the blockchain model used by Bitcoin.

It is important to understand that the Bitcoin model is not definitive of blockchain technology. Bitcoin demonstrates one implementation of this technology. There are several factors that make Bitcoin's blockchain work the way that it does, and it is worth examining each of them to get a fuller understanding of which aspects of Bitcoin's implementation of the blockchain are specific to Bitcoin and which are aspects of blockchain technology in general.

The Bitcoin Blockchain

There are several fundamental concepts that work together to create a blockchain ecosystem that is unique to Bitcoin. Other cryptocurrencies have implemented similar models, but for our purposes, it makes sense to zoom in on Bitcoin and break down how the Bitcoin blockchain works.

We already know that blockchains are a form of distributed ledger. If we dig a bit deeper into this idea of a distributed ledger, some questions that may arise are: how are transactions are verified? Who records them? How can we be sure this information is accurate?

Encryption

If you recall from the earlier section on the history of Bitcoin, you may remember that the concept was introduced initially to a popular cryptography mailing list. Why cryptography?

The field of cryptography has developed rapidly alongside digital technology as a way securing information. Cryptography has traditionally been a somewhat obscure field, historically used largely in military contexts. In the days of the Roman Empire, Julius Cesar famously used an encryption technique to send coded messages to his generals.

In the digital age, encryption has become a fundamental part of everyday life. As hacking and identity theft has become more and more prominent, basic encryption practices have entered the mainstream as protective measures for keeping one's personal data safe. Whether we are aware of it or not, most of us today are already familiar with basic encryption techniques, such as using passwords to access our email accounts or enabling two-factor authentication on our smartphones. Most rely on encrypted transactions on a regular basis, from making online purchases to accessing our bank accounts.

It should come as no surprise then, that Bitcoin relies on cryptographically secure algorithms to validate transactions and manage the blockchain.

Chapter 3: The SHA-256 Hashing Algorithm

Bitcoin uses a cryptographically secure SHA-256 hashing algorithm. While an in-depth explanation of exactly how this works is beyond the scope of this book, it is helpful to get a basic overview. One way to think of this is to imagine a black box. That box is the SHA-256 algorithm. For our purposes, we aren't really going to worry about what happens inside the box, the nuts – and - bolts of the algorithm itself. We will just proceed with the assumption that inside the box, mysterious mathematical things happen.

The important aspect, for us, is that you can take any kind of data, of any size, and feed it into the box. Ultimately all digital data, even complex things like movies that are many gigabytes in size, exist as a sequence of 1's and 0's, or "bits." When we feed any kind of data into the black box of SHA-256, the bits in that data are processed. We can think of the bits as being "rearranged" in a certain way inside the box. When the data has been processed by the black box, it spits out a 256-bit string of seemingly random characters, which looks like nonsense. We can think of this string like a unique "fingerprint" representing the exact data that we fed in.

Truth be told, the apparent "nonsense" that comes out is not actually nonsense. SHA-256 is determinative, which means that if you put the same data into the "black box", you will get the same exact output string, or "fingerprint", every single time. If you apply SHA-256 the word "hello" you will get the identical 64-character string as seen above.

Another feature of this hash function is that it is a one-way function. This means that you cannot take the output string and convert it back to the original data. So, in our example, we cannot reverse the process by using the "nonsense" to get back to the original "hello."

One example of how this is used is to verify documents, such as PDF's. If you sign a contract and send it to someone along with the SHA-256 fingerprint, they can test the hash to ensure that not a single bit of the data has been altered. If they feed the document into SHA-256 and get the identical output string, then the document has not been changed.

If, on the other hand, the slightest change has occurred-regardless of whether it was a well-intentioned modification such as a typo being fixed or a case of nefarious tampering -

the fingerprint that comes out will be completely different. The nature or scope of the change to the original data doesn't matter to the algorithm; the output of the SHA-256 algorithm will be totally different unless the data is 100% identical. For example, in the above example, if you change the word "hello" to "Hello" or "HELLO," you will get a totally different output string.

Now that we have a basic grasp on how SHA-256 works you might be wondering how this relates to the Bitcoin blockchain. This can be one of the more complicated concepts to grasp in terms of what goes on under the hood of Bitcoin's protocol. In order to understand the role of SHA-256 in the "Proof of Work" model that makes Bitcoin function, we need to dig a bit deeper into how Bitcoin miners participate in the blockchain ecosystem.

The Role of Bitcoin Miners

Many explanations of how Bitcoin transactions are verified say something akin to: "miners solve complicated math problems to add blocks to the chain in exchange for a reward." This is accurate, and it is a fine explanation in terms of getting the big picture. When it comes to understanding the larger architecture of blockchain technology as it applies to Bitcoin, however, we find that this explanation is a bit oversimplified. For our purposes, we need to explore the mechanics of Bitcoin mining a bit more closely.

Mining involves complex computation designed to find certain combinations of random numbers (called "nonces"). These nonces are combined with information about particular Bitcoin transactions to yield a SHA-256 string that meets very specific criteria.

Data concerning Bitcoin transactions are found in the header, or first "chunk" of any block on the blockchain, which is displayed as a SHA-256 string. So, the first "chunk" of the string that makes up each block contains information about the transactions contained in that block, such as the time, amount of Bitcoin, addresses involved, and other details. The remainder of the string is produced by finding a nonce that, when added to the transaction data, will produce a SHA-256 string that meets the aforementioned target criteria.

So, what are the criteria and who decides it? Bitcoin blocks need to be constructed according to a set of rules in order to be considered valid by the consensus model governing all "nodes" on the Bitcoin network. This rule set- the criteria that must be met to generate a valid block- is written into the core code of Bitcoin's software. The "rules" are a set of functions written into the C++ code that runs on every machine (or "node") that is connected to the Bitcoin network.

A miner needs to create a block following this set of rules. First, the block needs to include information about the most recent Bitcoin transactions. Then, the miner must find a nonce that, when added to the transaction data, will produce a SHA-256 string that meets the criteria set by Bitcoin's software (for example, the criteria might be something like the string must contain 15 zeroes in a row).

There is no way to find the nonce other than using a "brute force" method, which basically just means trial and error. Miners try a bunch of random numbers really quickly until they find one that works. When a miner "solves a block," it means that they have found a nonce that produces a SHA-256 hash that meets the criteria for a valid block. They can then submit their answer to the Bitcoin network and other nodes will check it and confirm that it is valid.

To give you an idea of how complicated it is to find the nonce, the Bitcoin network produces upwards of 500 quadrillion hashes per second. These are all attempts to find a nonce that produces the necessary result. Even with that massive amount of work, it still takes an average of 10 minutes to solve a block, or to find a viable nonce. When a miner does solve a block successfully, they are rewarded with a small amount of Bitcoin.

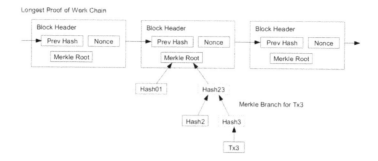

Longest Proof of Work Chain

By Satoshi Nakamoto - http://bitcoin.org/bitcoin.pdf, MIT, https://commons.wikimedia.org/w/index.php?curid=24542 868

(The "Merkle Root" is a reference to a mathematical concept called a Merkle Tree. In this case, the Merkle Root is the hash of all the transactions making up the block. The details of each individual transaction are also hashed, so the "Merkle Root" is actually the hash of all of those hashes.)

Bitcoin Miners Pay to Play

You may have heard people talk about Bitcoin mining as a way to make "free money." This has never been the case, even in the early days of Bitcoin, and it is even less so today as the complexity of solving blocks increases over time in correlation to the amount of Bitcoin in circulation.

The specificity of the SHA-256 string gets more complicated over time (this is known as the "difficulty target"), making the amount of power required to find a valid nonce more significant. Today, special equipment is needed to successfully mine Bitcoin in any sort of meaningful way, and even then most miners combine their resources into pools that share both the burden of work and the rewards.

Miners use their equipment to test hashes at an incredibly rapid rate. As you can imagine, this kind of computing power requires a lot of electricity, which is generally not free. The reason that the Bitcoin mining infrastructure works is due in part to the fact that to participate, miners incur a cost. Without the sacrifice, there is no reward. The only reason that someone would mine Bitcoin is that they believe the incentive is worth more than that hefty electric bill that comes from mining.

When a miner does find a nonce that works, their result will be checked and validated by the wider Bitcoin network. If it checks out, they have provided Proof of Work and can receive their reward. If the rest of the nodes on the Bitcoin network see that something in a proposed block does not meet the criteria, either by following a rule incorrectly or by failing to provide a nonce that meets the criteria, the block will be rejected and that miner will have just wasted money and resources. For example, if someone attempts to "double-spend," this will be caught and the block will be rejected.

Bitcoin's use of a Proof-of-Work consensus model makes it virtually impossible to cheat or hack the blockchain. With Bitcoin, miners pay to play, and it only pays to play fair. Not only that, but those who don't play fair will actually lose money due to the cost of electricity required to operate mining rigs.

Blockchain Beyond Bitcoin

When we look at the Bitcoin Blockchain, we can see that it is made up of several distinct parts that work together to create the overall architecture of the ecosystem. Three of the components that we have looked at thus far are the idea of a distributed ledger, the use of SHA-256, and a Proof-of-Work consensus model.

Which of these are unique to Bitcoin and which is baked into the concept of blockchain technology itself? That's a good question, and the answer may depend on whom you ask. There is some debate over where Bitcoin stops and blockchain begins, or rather what features of Bitcoin's blockchain are essential to creating other blockchains that actually work in a practical way.

On a basic level, when we remove the trappings of Bitcoin from the fundamental concept of a blockchain, we are left ultimately with the notion of a distributed ledger that contains a record of transactions. What kind of transactions and how they are handled, verified, and recorded is something that different blockchain applications may handle in different ways.

When we start to look into other implementations of blockchain technology, we need to look closely at how they function. How are they ensuring security? Are they open and accessible to anyone? Do they operate in a decentralized manner? How are they encrypting information? Are transactions anonymous? What kinds of transactions are being handled? Do they use Proof of Work? Is there another consensus model? These are all questions that arise when we begin to look at blockchain technology as it applies to spaces beyond Bitcoin.

Chapter 4: Cryptocurrency Beyond Bitcoin

Ethereum

The cryptocurrency space is notoriously volatile. Things change on a daily basis and new coins are being developed all the time. What is considered revolutionary one day can be obsolete the next. That being said there are some digital currencies that have achieved relative stability. Bitcoin is widely considered to be the leader in blockchain-based currencies, but Ethereum has gained a lot of traction since its inception in late 2013.

Ethereum was developed by the programmer Vitalik Buterin. Unlike Bitcoin, which functions solely as a digital currency, Ethereum is a blockchain-based platform for developing decentralized applications that run using "smart contracts." Where Bitcoin serves an electronic peer-to-peer cash system, the Ethereum blockchain runs the code making up decentralized applications.

It may be helpful to visualize Ethereum as similar to a smartphone. A smartphone comes with a general operating system, like iOS or Android. Anybody can create apps that do any number of different things to run on that operating system. Ethereum, in this analogy, is like the operating system: a framework to build upon.

One application that runs on Ethereum is a digital currency, which is often also referred to as "Ethereum," although technically it is called Ether. This can be confusing since both the currency and the platform are usually called "Ethereum," but it is important to remember that the currency is merely one aspect of the Ethereum blockchain framework. As a reward for maintaining the Ethereum blockchain, Ethereum "miners" are rewarded with Ether.

From its inception, Ethereum mining has worked on a Proof-of-Work consensus model similar to Bitcoin. As of 2017, however, the team behind Ethereum has announced plans to shift to a Proof-of-Stake model. Understanding the difference between these two systems of validating blockchain transactions is crucial to gaining context for some of the most pressing debates in the larger blockchain space today.

When we looked at "Proof of Work" as integral to the Bitcoin protocol, we covered how Bitcoin miners have to invest in special mining equipment that requires a lot of electricity to run in order to solve a block. Proof-of-Stake (PoS) works a bit differently.

A Proof-of-Stake model is a bit more like gambling. Rather than being called "miners," Ethereum is moving towards the term "validators." Validators stake a certain amount of their own money (Ether, in the case of Ethereum) towards solving a block. The more money a validator stakes, the higher the probability that they will solve the block.

The Proof-of-Stake model simulates the "work" involved with performing meaningless calculations, which thus reduces the real environmental impact of energy consumption created via mining. We know that validators stake their funds towards solving a block, like placing a bet, but what happens if someone tries to "cheat"?

In Ethereum's Proof-of-Stake algorithm (called Casper), what will happen, in the event of a bad actor, is that the funds belonging to anyone trying to do something nefarious will simply disappear! The system will erase them out of circulation. So, the incentive for a validator to participate in earnest is high, and the consequences for trying to "validate" a false transaction are high.

The Proof-of-Work and Proof-of-Stake models both ultimately strive for the same outcome: they want to validate blocks and add those blocks to the blockchain in such a way that the broader network is in consensus about the validity of those blocks. Both models, ideally, will achieve the same result through a different protocol.

As a potential investor and/or participant in the blockchain space, becoming familiar with different consensus models is a good way to deepen your understanding of how projects function in the real world. The shift in Ethereum's model from Proof-of-Work based on mining to Proof-of-Stake based on validation will further set Ethereum apart from Bitcoin in terms of its structure, but it is also worth examining some of the other ways in which these two technologies are already fundamentally quite different.

We have already mentioned that Ethereum, while it is a currency in part, is primarily a platform for developing decentralized applications. The idea of decentralized applications (often called "dApps") can be a little bit confusing, largely because it is a really new way of organizing information. Why do we need a blockchain-based platform to run applications? This is actually a question that many programmers are still exploring the answers to. One answer, however, has to do with a concept that is referred to in the world of programming as "state."

"State" basically just refers to the status of any given application or program at a certain point in time. One of the things that makes Ethereum's blockchain different than Bitcoin's is that "transactions" that happen on the Ethereum blockchain can actually trigger code to be executed. So, programs can be triggered to run as a result of transactions that happen on the Ethereum platform. Each time something changes within an application, that application's state changes. The Ethereum blockchain keeps a record of every state change that occurs within an application. For example, a smart contract can be paid when work is delivered entirely through the Ethereum blockchain.

If you're feeling a little bit lost, don't worry. Unless you plan on developing applications on the Ethereum platform, you really don't need to understand the technical aspects of state change. That being said, it is worth becoming familiar with these concepts if you plan to get involved in the blockchain space as an investor or entrepreneur. To get a better idea of what Ethereum is capable of, it let's look at one of the decentralized apps being developed on the Ethereum platform.

Golem

Golem is one popular project based on the Ethereum framework. The idea is fairly simple. A lot of people have computers. A lot of people who have computers don't use them all of the time, and even when they are using them they often don't use them to their full capacity in terms of processing power. At the same time, there are a lot of fields where massive amounts of computing power are required to accomplish certain tasks. For example, rendering video is very costly in terms of computing power. It takes a long time and it can be pretty slow on a slow machine. Many scientific studies also require computationally intensive data analysis and other forms of high-level computer processing.

The Golem project is designed to allow people to essentially rent out their unused computer processing power to people who need it for projects. Using a decentralized structure, this means that people from all over the world can contribute small amounts of their computer power towards completing a computationally intensive task that would normally require a very powerful computer to accomplish.

By using a blockchain-based framework that allows for code to be executed when transactions occur, i.e. Ethereum, Golem is working towards creating what are essentially decentralized supercomputers that are accessible to anyone. Because the entire history of a program's state is recorded on the Ethereum blockchain, participants can ensure that nobody is using more power than they have paid for and vice-versa, as well as ensure other features concerning their transactions.

Golem also has its own digital currency, based on Ether, through which participants can buy and sell their resources, and, of course, which anyone can invest in regardless of whether or not they are participating in the project directly. Golem is widely considered to be one of the more popular and successful applications built on the Ethereum platform as of the time of this writing.

Ripple

We've already covered some of the ways in which Ethereum differs from Bitcoin. One thing that we have not yet noted is that Ethereum, unlike Bitcoin, is managed by a central team of known people. This group determines what happens with Ethereum, such as the move from Proof-of-Work to Proof-of-Stake, and therefore exercises a certain level of control over the platform in a way that is more centralized than Bitcoin.

Even so, Ethereum is still an open blockchain platform, accessible to anyone.

Ripple is another example of a variation on blockchain technology. Ripple is twofold: both a cryptocurrency and a technology company in the blockchain space. Ripple's focus is less on peer-to-peer transactions and more on the financial industry itself, partnering with banks and financial institutions to integrate blockchain technology into their infrastructure.

Ripple remains somewhat controversial amongst cryptocurrency enthusiasts, but it does claim to solve some of the problems posed by Bitcoin. Most significantly, Ripple eliminates the waiting period associated with verification. Transactions can happen instantly. However, Ripple's consensus model differs from Bitcoin's "Proof of Work" model and instead relies on a centralized network of "trusted" servers, which poses some big questions for those whose interest in blockchain technology lies in the promise of decentralized architecture.

The concept of a distributed ledger as it is implemented via blockchain technology represents a fundamental reimagining of institutional organizations from a hierarchical model to a distributed network. For many investors, this is the key to the revolutionary potential of blockchain technology. The implications of decentralizing information are significant, and almost certainly have not yet been fully realized.

Chapter 5: Implications of Blockchain: Big Data, Privacy, and Personal Data

As we enter an increasingly digital age, many of the practices that were developed prior to the Internet have simply been applied to the new framework of a networked world. Instead of writing letters, we now send e-mails, for example. At face value, the process doesn't seem that all that different. In some cases, it isn't.

Regardless of how you may feel about it, there is no denying that more and more things are becoming integrated into the Internet, hence the aptly titled notion of the "Internet of Things" (often abbreviated to IoT). Devices like heart-rate monitors, self-driving cars, and even refrigerators are making their way into the market. Of course, almost everyone is already accustomed to carrying a smartphone around at all times, regularly checking GPS information, updating social media feeds, managing financial transactions, and much more.

Almost every area of life that one can think of is wired into the web already or has the potential to be in the near future. While there are many advantages to the burgeoning revolution in "smart technology," there are also some major concerns and challenges.

While it may seem like things like social media networks, smart toasters, and FitBits are entirely different ideas, they actually have quite a bit in common. Fundamentally, they all produce data: data about you. If you recall in the section on SHA-256, we noted that all digital data can ultimately be reduced to 0's and 1's. From that perspective, our heart rate and our Google search history are not ultimately all that different in terms. We all generate data constantly, whether it is telling Amazon's Alexa to order more paper towels, Googling pictures of baby sea lions, or tracking your workout schedule with an App or a wearable.

Where does this data go? Who owns this data? What can be learned about you by your trail of data? These questions quickly lead anyone bold enough to ask them into very uncomfortable territory. While getting to deep into the answer to this particular set of questions is beyond the scope of this book, it is worth scratching the surface. In short, there are huge multi-national companies that buy up your data and sell it to other companies. What do they do with it? Good question. Of course, they target ads based on your history. Sure. We all know that. What else, though? Part of what makes this avenue uncomfortable is that nobody really knows, and the space of data collection is loosely defined and loosely regulated.

Let's look at an example. Let's say, hypothetically, you found a little lump in your armpit one day. You are naturally a bit nervous, and you rush over to Google and spend several hours clicking around different websites to read articles about cancer. Now, let's say, hypothetically, that whatever company is sucking up your data gets their hands on this searching binge. Perhaps they also notice that you looked up a phone number for some doctor in the area who does cancer screenings. While you're at it, maybe it is time to start thinking about your health insurance policy, or to buy life insurance just in case?

Continuing the hypothetical situation, if an insurance provider were to buy your data, already parsed by some massive data broker, and see that you had been recently looking up information about cancer, what are the implications? Even if you have told nobody about the lump, even if you have not been evaluated by a doctor or diagnosed, could this potential insurer infer things from your data history when deciding on your premium rate, or whether to offer insurance to you at all?

This is just one example of a wide range of ethical and legal dilemmas that arise when we really begin thinking about the implications of our data, how it is mined, who "owns it," and who has access to it.

The more integrated technology becomes into society and all levels of life and the more pervasive networks become, the greater the volume and variety of data about all of us. What movies and music we stream, our shopping history, political leanings, sexual preferences, connections on social networks, dcvices we use, and much more is information that is often being collected as a result of blindly checking a user agreement box in order to use a particular service.

Ok, that's creepy, but what does it have to do with blockchain technology? Good question. The relationship between privacy and technology is an issue that spans many industries and contemporary debates.

For many enthusiasts of both cryptocurrencies and blockchain technology, privacy is a major concern. When it comes to the concept of "privacy," many observers, including major media outlets, make the assumption that "the only people who care about privacy are those with something to hide." This has led to a great deal of reporting on cryptocurrencies, in particular, suggesting that the primary appeal of these technologies is that they enable criminal activity. As more and more areas of life become connected to the Internet, it seems far-fetched to suggest that desiring more control over one's personal data, transactions, and asset management constitutes or implies criminal behavior. Many privacy advocates argue that privacy is essential to both individual welfare and a functional democracy.

Rather than relying on centralized institutions to provide services in exchange for ownership of our data, blockchain-based models are beginning to emerge that shift information to a secure, trustless, decentralized structure. ("Trustless" here means that participants do not need to put their trust in a centralized institution to mediate transactions, keep records, distribute wealth, store data, etc.).

The implications for blockchain in spaces like managing personal information, such as health records, are extremely promising and beginning to gain a lot of attention from investors, entrepreneurs, major corporations, and government entities.

Regardless of your feelings on the subject of privacy, it is worth noting, from an investment perspective, that several notable cryptocurrencies have emerged with an emphasis on privacy as a defining factor. The ability to make completely anonymous transactions that are also totally secure has elevated several currencies to the forefront of the cryptocurrency space, including Monero, ZCash, and Dash. While none of these have reached quite the height of Bitcoin or Ethereum in terms of widespread adoption, all three of these are among the top 50 cryptocurrencies in terms of market value. We can infer from their success that enough people see value in anonymity to make these currencies competitive players in the larger cryptocurrency market, as well as the general blockchain space.

Profiting from Blockchain Technologies

It is important to remember that blockchain technology is still very new. The implications of secure distributed ledgers and decentralized peer-to-peer systems of this variety are not yet fully realized. As with any frontier space, even in the digital realm, there are a lot of opportunities. Of course, the nature of frontiers is that they are unexplored territory, and where there is potential for opportunity there is also a higher risk factor than one might encounter in tamer and more regulated environments.

While much of the blockchain space is a "wild west," major players and industry leaders from numerous fields are beginning to invest in and explore blockchain technology. Big technology companies such as IBM and Microsoft are beginning to explore blockchains, along with numerous banks, particularly in Europe and Asia.

Even governments in many parts of the world are beginning to implement blockchains to manage public services and records. Estonia, for example, issues citizens cryptographically secure ID cards, managed by a blockchain, that allow access to various public services. The government of Georgia is using blockchain technology to manage land titles and validate property transactions. The UN recently completed a trial program using the Ethereum blockchain to manage distribution of food aid to 10,000 refugees.

Over the past few years, numerous hedge funds dealing in cryptocurrencies and blockchain applications have sprung up all over the world, and many Wall Street speculators have fixed their attention on the blockchain space. In 2016, Overstock, one of the largest online retailers in the US, released a blockchain-based platform for equities trading. Numerous startups have emerged that use blockchains to manage peer-to-peer micropayments at extremely low rates. In some cases, these enable international transfers and access to cash pickups, which allows unbanked individuals to send and receive payments.

New developments are happening on a daily basis in the blockchain space. For those interested in diving in, getting involved and profiting from these emerging technologies, the single most important thing you can do is to stay informed: Read white papers, join online communities, and explore the different projects gaining traction around blockchain technology. The more familiar you are with the space, the easier it will be to make informed decisions about which projects to invest in.

As a practical matter, broadly speaking, there are two general directions you can go in terms of investing in blockchain technology: cryptocurrencies and everything else. These are by no means mutually exclusive, and as we have seen with projects like Ethereum and Ripple, there is often some overlap between the two, or the integration of a digital token into a particular blockchain application.

Within the cryptocurrency space, active online marketplaces and exchanges exist with a trading culture similar to traditional stock exchanges. People trade fiat currency for cryptocurrencies as well as trading one cryptocurrency for another, striving to make a profit by investing in currencies that they think will increase in value.

Most cryptocurrency exchanges deal primarily in Bitcoin. In order to buy into other cryptocurrencies, you almost always need to have some Bitcoin to exchange, although some currencies and exchanges allow for a direct exchange between fiat and "altcoins," a common term for cryptocurrencies other than Bitcoin. You can buy Bitcoin through several online exchanges or from an increasing number of Bitcoin ATM's that are available in various locations throughout the world.

You may choose to actively trade between different cryptocurrencies, or simply buy into Bitcoin and/or altcoins that you believe are promising and hold on to them with the assumption that they will increase in value over time. This is one way to get involved with what is currently the most active environment for blockchain applications. If you're lucky, you could end up as an "early investor" in a technology that really takes off.

Many people have entered the cryptocurrency space with precisely that hope, especially after hearing about the success of Bitcoin. If you are new to blockchain-based digital currencies, it is important to understand that this is an extremely volatile space. It is not uncommon to see huge spikes and drops in value throughout the course of a few hours, while it is possible to make a lot of money if you play your cards right, it is also easy to lose money.

Being aware of the risks and making smart investments in cryptocurrencies is arguably the most direct route towards profiting from blockchain technology. It is certainly the easiest. For people that don't necessarily have much capital to invest, the prospect of mining can sound pretty appealing. We've already discussed some of the challenges associated with mining Bitcoin: you need to buy specialized equipment, electricity costs, the need for massive computing power, etc. If you're low on capital, investing in a Bitcoin mining operation is probably not the best option.

However, there are many other cryptocurrencies that can be mined with considerably less of a barrier to entry. For those who are willing to learn what it takes to convert a spare computer into a mining rig, the ability to earn coins through mining can be a potential way to generate passive income through validating blockchain transactions.

Blockchain technology originated in the cryptocurrency space, and much of the early development of blockchain applications has been in relation to digital assets and financial transactions. In terms of profiting from blockchain technology, becoming involved with cryptocurrencies is one popular avenue, but it is not the only gig in town. Increasingly, as blockchain finds its way into new fields, a savvy investor can find many fascinating offshoots that could very well grow into massive projects with global implications and take the future by storm. Investing in companies, developers, and technology that are exploring the possibilities of blockchain is gaining rapid popularity with everyone from Silicon Valley entrepreneurs to Wall Street executives.

Of course, nobody knows for certain which blockchain-based application will be "the next Google." Any potential investor will inevitably face the challenge of gauging which initiatives are over-hyped versus which are promising underdogs, which are revolutionary platforms versus cheap imitations. While there is no crystal ball that can predict the future, you can bolster your odds of picking a winner by doing research and asking the right questions. Some important questions to ask when considering whether a project has a good chance of success include:

- What problem does the technology solve (Does incorporating a blockchain actually make sense in this situation? Is this the best solution?)

- Is this project actually functional? Is it live and being used currently or is it an idea that has not yet been built? If it hasn't been built, how can you be sure that it will actually accomplish what it promises?

- How is the blockchain structured? (For example, if the founder controls 90% of the nodes on the network, what might that say about the company?)

- What is their consensus algorithm? Proof-of-Work? Proof-of-Stake? Something else? Why did they choose this system and how is it implemented.

- Is it scalable? Could this system meet the demands of a large user base?

- How does anonymity factor into this application? Is that significant?

- Is this platform secure? How is security guaranteed? Is there "trust" involved in a centralized body? What kind of encryption are they using?

- Is the blockchain open and visible to anybody?

- Is the project's code open-source? (If it's not, why not? How will we be able to determine how decisions are made, transactions are deemed valid, and exactly what is being executed when we use this platform?)

- Who is behind this project? Is the development team qualified and reputable? Have they been involved with previous projects that failed? Why did those fail?

- Are other projects doing something similar? What makes this one the best?

- Do you believe in this project? Are you excited about it?

This laundry list of questions is by no means exhaustive, but if you are thinking about investing serious money in blockchain technology these considerations are a good place to begin. With the increasing attention of several major industries aimed towards blockchain technology, it should not come as a surprise that many entrepreneurs have taken notice of the potential for big money in developing blockchain applications. Needless to say, not all of these applications are going to succeed and some are more promising than others. Some projects can be noble efforts that simply don't have the best solution to a common problem; others may be outright scams.

Take time to become familiar with the buzzwords and jargon of the blockchain space. When a new company claims to deliver a blockchain platform that is "100% scalable," a wise investor will likely ask exactly how they have managed to accomplish this, rather than taking the company's word at face value. More often than not, you may find that bold claims like "100% scalable" are closer to "future goals" than to the current reality.

It is no secret that marketing hype can play a huge role in how "popular" something becomes. Cryptocurrencies and blockchain-based companies are no exception, and marketing can have a real impact on how a player in this space is valued. Maybe a project lives up to the hype, but it is generally a good idea to approach potential investments in this space with a dose of healthy skepticism. Alternatively, some of the most innovative and promising blockchain initiatives may be tiny start-ups with small budgets that do not have fancy websites and are not getting a huge amount of public attention.

By staying informed, looking at a wide variety of projects, figuring out which problems you think could be most successfully solved by blockchain technology, and gaining exposure to alternative points of view you can develop an in-depth understanding of the blockchain space. While there are no guarantees when it comes to investing, knowing what to look for goes a long way towards helping you will make smart decisions. Blockchain is still in the early days, and making smart decisions now definitely has the potential to lead to major profits.

Limitations & Challenges of Blockchain

Speed

One of the biggest challenges facing Bitcoin, and other blockchains using a Proof-of-Work model based on Bitcoin, is speed. Because mining a block is so resource intensive and involves so much trial and error in terms of finding the proper nonce to solve a block, it takes around 10 minutes for every new block to be mined.

Not only does this utilize a massive amount of electricity, but it also means that transactions are not verified instantaneously. In fact, it can take quite awhile to see your transaction move from "pending" to "verified". As a practical matter, this makes it difficult to buy something with Bitcoin in many situations. Most people don't want to wait around at a store for an hour while their transaction goes through. Furthermore, most merchants don't want to wait to see their money come through.

Despite this issue, the number of vendors willing to accept Bitcoin is growing on a daily basis. As more implementations of blockchain technology develop, different approaches are being taken to handle the speed of transaction and verification. Ripple, for example, offers instantaneous transactions but many critics have concerns about the centralization of the underlying protocol backing the technology that makes this kind of speed possible.

As a potential investor in a new technology, it is important to ask both how this is being addressed and examine whether security is being sacrificed to maximize speed. This is certainly not always the case, but it is something to watch out for when looking into new blockchain frameworks.

Scaling

Scaling is another one of the most notable issues currently facing blockchain implementations. If you visualize the blockchain exactly as it sounds, as a long chain of blocks, you can imagine that as more transactions occur and more blocks are added the chain, the chain gets longer and longer.

Part of what makes a blockchain work is that multiple copies of it are stored and updated across a decentralized network. In theory, when a chain gets bigger, it will inevitably take up more and more space. If a chain were to get so big that it required a huge amount of storage space, those who didn't have ample room to store the chain would no longer be able to participate in the network. Thus, over time, only giant servers would suffice to store the enormous chain, leading us back the very sort of centralized model that blockchain technology was ultimately designed to avoid.

Scaling is a major problem that is being addressed in a variety of ways by innovators in the cryptocurrency and blockchain space. The "Lightning Network" is one method that has been introduced as a promising potential solution to current scaling problems faced by blockchain applications.

The Lightning Network works by allowing peer-to-peer micro-transactions to happen instantaneously using blockchain smart contracts, but without adding individual transactions to the main blockchain. The Lightning Network also supports "atomic swaps" between different blockchains, i.e. from one cryptocurrency to another, so long as those chains support the same cryptographic hash functions. By combining the Bitcoin blockchain with its own, in-house, scripting language to manage smart contracts, the Lightning Network is one example of a blockchain-based solution to the problem of blockchain scaling. This is one example of how this technology builds upon itself to develop new implementations on top of the existing architecture.

Quantum computing

Quantum computers might sound like science fiction, but they are not far from becoming a reality. Without getting into the "how" of quantum computing, what we need to look at in relation to blockchain technology is the "what." What does quantum computing mean for us, generally, and what are the implications for blockchain tech?

In a nutshell, the promise of quantum computing is incredible speed and incredible power. As of now, if we look at the example of Bitcoin, we know that blocks are "mined" by a decentralized network of machines that work to verify Bitcoin transactions by solving complex math problems in exchange for a small amount of Bitcoin. When the problem is solved and the transaction is verified, a block is added to the chain.

Quantum computers would be able to solve these math problems at a rate infinitely faster than anything currently in existence. That's problem number one.

Problem number two arises when we think about the model of majority consensus that governs the Bitcoin protocol. In order to modify the blockchain, one would have to alter the record on over 50% of copies stored all around the world. Today, the kind of processing power required to do that makes hacking the blockchain effectively impossible. Quantum computing has the potential to change that, although at the moment this risk remains theoretical.

Chapter 6: The Human Touch: Or, The 51% Problem

One of the central pillars of blockchain technology is the ability to conduct transactions in a trustless environment without needing a "middle-man." In laymen's terms, we ultimately put our trust in an unbiased mathematical process carried out by computers rather than in human beings. We are guaranteed a form of security that is theoretically as free as possible from human tampering.

Of course, it is impossible to discount human beings completely. The power of a decentralized application that relies on computational verification marks a significant paradigm shift from a top-down hierarchy towards a distributed network. However, when we look at the Bitcoin blockchain we can see that the consensus model requires a majority to agree in order to verify a block. 51% of miners constitute a majority.

What happens if, as the expenses of mining increase along with the ever-growing blockchain, miners consolidate their influence into larger and larger pools? This concern is not entirely theoretical. As of the time of this writing, almost 50% of all Bitcoin blocks are estimated to be mined by two large mining pools.

To execute what is known as a "51% attack," a single entity would have to contribute 51% or more of the entire Bitcoin networks mining hashrate. This would require an almost unfathomable amount of computer power, which would equate to an equally unfathomable electricity cost. Realistically, most governments do not even possess the resources to execute a 51% attack on Bitcoin. It would be incredibly difficult, but it is not necessarily impossible. If it did happen, the attacker would not really be able to take complete control over the network. They would be able to prevent new transactions from being validated, but they could not reverse transactions that were already recorded on the blockchain, steal Bitcoins from other people's wallets or create new Bitcoins at will.

The 51% problem is something that any decentralized structure built on a similar model will need to contend with. Some advocates of Proof-of-Stake consensus suggest that this model offers more robust security against a 51% attack.

All emerging industries and new technologies face challenges, and blockchains are no exception. An entire generation of entrepreneurs, developers, and professionals is emerging in the blockchain space, and for those who believe in the revolutionary potential of this technology, it is a land of opportunity.

The Future of Blockchain

We've covered several foundational concepts throughout the course of this book in relation to blockchain technology. As the world becomes more and more interconnected through networked technology, and the amount of data we generate grows in both quantity and form, there is an increasing demand and opportunity for new models of organization to handle the interface of digital and material life. Blockchain's usage of a distributed ledger and the potential for creating decentralized rather than hierarchical structures in a way that is secure, trustless, and open marks a revolutionary step towards reimagining the way many of today's dominant institutions operate.

As with any new technology, there are competing ideologies, varying implementations, and a number of challenges that are present in the blockchain space. Whether the Bitcoin blockchain will continue to be the dominant blockchain model and Bitcoin will continue as the most popular cryptocurrency is something that only time will tell. There is, undoubtedly, a lot of room to grow when it comes to realizing the full potential of blockchain technology in terms of creating institutional transparency, decentralized networks, peer-to-peer transactions, asset management, and much more. Industries ranging from healthcare, finance, and social media to retail, airlines, and manufacturing have all begun to explore the potential for integrating with blockchain-based systems. Governments, banks, and organizations have already begun to implement blockchain systems to manage transactions, access to public services, and the distribution of humanitarian aid.

Whether you are excited by the ideological implications of decentralized networks radically transforming the landscape of hierarchical institutions on a global scale or you are an investor eager to get on board with the next big thing, blockchain technology is markedly promising. Blockchain is unquestionably the way of the future. Despite the huge uptick in interest in blockchain technology over the past few years, we are still very much in the early stages of this space. Even if you're completely new to blockchain today, in five or ten years you could very likely be considered an "early adopter" of most disruptive technology since the advent of the Internet.

Ethereum

The year 2017 has seen a marked increase in general awareness and interest in digital currencies, such as Bitcoin, as well as the underlying technology driving this new economy, known as "blockchain." Major industries ranging from healthcare to finance, governmental agencies, and a wide variety of startups are beginning to explore the potential for blockchain technology to radically reshape the landscape of institutional structures.

There are generally two things that draw most people to the space of blockchain tech and cryptocurrencies. The first is money. Many people have heard the story of Bitcoin's rapid rise from having almost no value to being worth thousands of dollars over the course of a few short years. Naturally, everybody who hears about this today wishes that they had known about Bitcoin sooner and had invested in the early days. Of course, it makes sense that this would provoke anyone to look further into the cryptocurrency space in hopes of finding "another Bitcoin." This is how many people first become acquainted with Ethereum.

The second reason that people generally tend to be drawn to the cryptocurrency space is an interest in the technology. There is a great deal of potential for blockchain-based applications to reshape various industries, institutions, and social structures. Of course, these two broad interests, money and new technology, are not mutually exclusive. After all, who doesn't want to change the world and get rich at the same time?

Regardless of where your initial interest in Ethereum comes from, it is important to understand Ethereum as both a currency and a technology. In this book, we will explore what this means and how Ethereum works, both as a digital asset and as a platform for building blockchain-based applications.

As we begin to explore Ethereum, it is important to note that many people refer to the Ethereum currency as "Ethereum." Technically, the currency unit is known as "Ether." Ether is one component of the much larger framework of "Ethereum." For the sake of clarity, we will use the term "Ether" in reference to the currency from now own, although in the real world you may see it called both Ether and/or Ethereum. As we progress through this book, the importance of recognizing the distinction between these two entities will become clearer.

Whether you plan to simply invest in Ether as a currency or you want to build a revolutionary application on the Ethereum platform, it is critical to understand the role of both the currency and the larger framework. In the cryptocurrency space, as of today, Ether is second only to Bitcoin in terms of popularity and value. In a few short years, it has gained considerable traction and become a forerunner in the burgeoning blockchain revolution.

Throughout this book, we will examine Ethereum's distinct approach to blockchain technology as a technological framework for building decentralized applications. We will cover what this means, how these applications work, and what you need to know if you're thinking about investing in Ether, a project built on the Ethereum platform, or even developing your own Ethereum-based application.

Chapter 1: A Brief History of Ethereum

The initial concept for Ethereum was introduced in the year 2013, detailed in a white paper written by Russian-Canadian programmer Vitalik Buterin. Buterin, only 19 years old at the time, had already been was involved with Bitcoin for several years. In 2014, he received the Theil Fellowship and was awarded $100,000, which prompted him to go drop out of college and dedicate himself full-time to developing Ethereum.

As an active participant in the cryptocurrency space, Buterin saw the potential for extending the blockchain structure beyond Bitcoin. The initial vision for the Ethereum project was to create a platform to develop decentralized applications with broad capabilities. Simply put, Buterin envisioned possibilities for a Bitcoin-like system that could be used for more than just one kind of peer-to-peer financial transactions. Buterins ultimate vision for Ethereum can be viewed as an earnest attempt to apply learnings from Bitcoin's decentralized, global cryptographic network to challenges beyond mere value exchange. Rather than just cutting out the middleman and simply sending and receiving money, the programmers saw the bigger picture and saw the possibility of using "bitcoins" to represent commodities, derivatives or even deeds to real estate – Pretty much anything for which a secure, fixed unit of code could function as a digital asset.

In essence, Buterin envisioned how the platform could remove the conventional arbitrators of trust and in turn enable a new wave of application development – one that could possibly change the way we carry out "trusted" transactions without the use of outdated, painstaking slow legal systems that are in place today.

By 2014, Ethereum had established a core team of developers, gained considerable support, and was officially under development. A crowd-sale of the initial round of Ether, the digital currency used by Ethereum, took place in July-August of 2014, with proceeds funding further development of the software.

On July 30, 2015, the first iteration of Ethereum officially went live. Today, Ethereum is still maintained by a central team of developers, including founder Vitalik Buterin, and is managed by a Swiss non-profit organization called the Ethereum Foundation. Unlike Bitcoin, whose creator remains a mystery, Buterin serves as a figurehead for this project and his identity is very much tied to Ethereum. While there are many other programmers and thinkers contributing to the development of Ethereum, Buterin is generally viewed as the inventor and the "face" of the project. Some critics have expressed concern over the centrality of the Ethereum project and a "cult of personality" surrounding Buterin.

Throughout its short history, Ethereum has provoked international interest, gained a lot of support, and received its fair share of criticism, as well. Ether, as a currency, despite periods of volatility, has become one of the more valuable digital currencies in the cryptocurrency space.

Particularly because it is such a new technology, it is impossible to predict what the future holds for the Ethereum platform. Throughout 2016 and 2017, we have seen a huge uptick in global interest in cryptocurrencies and the concept of blockchain technology across many industries and institutions. The Ethereum platform represents, for many, the closest thing that currently exists to a framework for building decentralized blockchain applications capable of running autonomously. At the same time, Ethereum is still in its early stages. Many argue that it has not yet reached the level of stability, security and scalability necessary to usher in the future of blockchain and decentralized applications.

Throughout this book, we will explore the capabilities, potential, and challenges presented by Ethereum. We will take a broad look at the concepts and practical applications of this new technology. It is important to understand that many of the underlying aspects of Ethereum, particularly when looking at critiques and the roadmap for development, are highly technical.

While getting into the code itself and many of the mathematical concepts under the hood of the Ethereum platform is beyond the scope of this book, we will zoom in on the foundational ideas and explore the practical questions:

What is it? How does it work? How can I use it? We will explore the fundamental differences between Bitcoin and Ethereum, and look at some real-world examples of how Ethereum is being used to develop new kinds of applications.

Chapter 2: An Overview of Blockchain Technology

Before we begin to dig into the specifics of Ethereum, it is crucial to understand some of the core principles of blockchain technology, in general. For newcomers to the cryptocurrency space, one of the concepts that can be initially quite confusing is the relationship between cryptocurrencies and blockchain.

Blockchain technology is the underlying force behind both Bitcoin and Ethereum, but these two projects use this technology in different ways. To understand how Ethereum implements the blockchain, however, it is helpful to have some background in Bitcoin.

Bitcoin was the first digital currency and the first application built on a blockchain platform. Today, Bitcoin is by far the most popular and well-known cryptocurrency, as well as the largest, active open blockchain in the world. As Bitcoin began to enter into the mainstream, many media outlets developed a tendency to (incorrectly) use the term "Bitcoin" and "blockchain" almost interchangeably. Even today, many articles can be found that struggle to clearly elucidate the relationship between Bitcoin, other cryptocurrencies, and blockchain technology.

For the sake of clarity, let's break down the fundamentals. Bitcoin is fundamentally a currency. It was designed to enable digital, secure, peer-to-peer financial transactions and it has been, for the most part, highly successful in achieving this specific goal. Bitcoin uses a blockchain to perform its function. Blockchain technology, on the other hand, has implications that extend far beyond Bitcoin, and far beyond the realm of digital currencies, in general.

The blockchain model upon which Bitcoin is built works very well for Bitcoin, albeit with some areas for improvement. (For example, Bitcoin transactions can take a long time to be approved, which presents a barrier to entry for many merchants in terms of accepting payment in Bitcoin. Nobody wants to wait around in a store for an hour while a Bitcoin transaction is being verified).

While Bitcoin was the first technology to implement the blockchain, early adopters, like Vitalik Buterin, quickly began to see the potential for blockchain architecture in a wide variety of other environments. Because Bitcoin was designed specifically to be a currency, innovators began to explore the question of whether the particular blockchain structure employed by Bitcoin was the best model upon which to build other applications, beyond peer-to-peer transactions of a digital currency. Ethereum was born from this idea of creating a more flexible environment for deploying the power of blockchain technology in a universal way, across a broad spectrum of different applications.

So, what is a blockchain is and how does it work? To truly

answer this question in depth would require trudging through some fairly advanced mathematical concepts that are a bit beyond the scope of this book. Fortunately, unless you plan on becoming a programmer, you don't really need to understand the nitty-gritty of cryptographic hashing algorithms in order to get a solid grasp of the broader concepts and structure of blockchain.

Blockchains do use complex math, but if we zoom out they are ultimately fairly simple to understand from a bird's eye view. Starting with the terminology, we have "blocks" that are linked together, one after another, to form a "chain." Each block is made up of some kind of data related to events that took place during a particular period of time. The most recent block contains data pertaining to the most recent events. In the case of Bitcoin, this data is transaction data, such as the addresses of the Bitcoin wallets sending and receiving funds, the amount of coin being transacted, the time of the transactions, and other such details.

So, each new block is a collection of a bunch of data about the most recent transactions that have taken place. Each block is linked to the previous block with a special kind of cryptographically secure time stamp. Some complex math stuff happens here to make sure that any new block matches up with the entire history of all previous transactions on the entire blockchain.

Each new timestamp must match up with the previous block's timestamp, which in turn linked to the one before that, thus creating a long chain where each block is verifiably connected to the previous one, all the way back to the very first block, known as the "genesis block." The entire history of every single Bitcoin transaction that has ever occurred is recorded on the blockchain, which is publicly available for anyone to look at. The potential for secure transactions with this level of transparency is a feature that has drawn many people to Bitcoin and to blockchain technology.

Simply put, the Bitcoin blockchain is ultimately just a record of every single verified Bitcoin transaction that has ever happened. Transactions that happen in a given period of time are grouped together in blocks. Multiple, identical copies of the blockchain are stored and updated constantly by a big network of participating computers all over the world. This is what is known as a "distributed ledger." A distributed ledger is fundamentally just a giant decentralized database, or a record of information, events or transactions. Decentralization is a core concept behind the blockchain architecture of both Bitcoin and Ethereum, as well as many other blockchain-based initiatives and cryptocurrencies.

Not all distributed ledgers are blockchains, but all blockchains use some kind of distributed ledger system. Usually, this means that identical copies are stored and updated simultaneously on many different machines all over the world. In the case of Bitcoin, for anyone to hack or "cheat" the blockchain, they would have to manipulate the data of not only one block, but the entire historical record, on the majority of the entire network of decentralized machines, all at the same time. The kind of computational power required to do this makes it virtually impossible under current conditions, thus making the system secure by design.

Conceptually, while not totally identical, the Ethereum blockchain is structured in much the same way. The fundamental difference, when looking at Ethereum, is the kind of data that is being stored in blocks and the way that data is handled.

Chapter 3: The Ethereum Blockchain

Today, Bitcoin continues to be the largest, open public blockchain and serve as the definitive model upon which many other blockchain-based applications are based. However, the Bitcoin blockchain is only one implementation of blockchain technology. As more and more industries begin to explore the potential of blockchain, new models are emerging on a regular basis, often suited to serve a specific purpose.

When we look at Bitcoin, we see that fundamentally its purpose is a decentralized, peer-to-peer digital currency. Bitcoin solves a particular problem: how to make secure financial transactions on a peer-to-peer basis from anywhere in the world while eliminating the need for trust, a middleman, or centralized authority like a bank. While Bitcoin is not perfect, it has been quite successful in terms of serving the purpose for which it was intended.

As developers and entrepreneurs began to see implications for blockchain technology that went far beyond financial transactions, many began to imagine alternative blockchain structures that might be more suited to accomplish different functions. Vitalik Buterin, the developer who invented Ethereum, envisioned an open platform upon which anybody could build a blockchain-based application to perform any kind of function.

Rather than a blockchain that simply stored financial transaction data, as with Bitcoin, the Ethereum blockchain is designed to execute code based on verified transactions. Instead of simply moving funds from Account A to Account B, as with Bitcoin, Ethereum could create an environment where a transaction from Account A to Account B could trigger a vast range of events. For example, transactions in Ethereum can be used to register a new domain name, transfer property titles, manage voter registration, or execute secure contracts between two or more parties. In fact, "transactions" within Ethereum are often referred to as "smart contracts."

Chapter 4: Smart Contracts in Ethereum

The term "Smart Contracts" comes up a lot in reference to Ethereum. What is a smart contract? The short answer is that a smart contract is a computer program. Smart contracts are really the "meat and potatoes" of Ethereum, and it is worth exploring this concept in some depth in order to really grasp the power and vision of the platform.

If you don't have much in the way of technical background, don't worry. When it comes to actually writing smart contracts you will need to learn to code or hire a programmer, but you don't need to know how to code in order to understand, conceptually, how smart contracts work. However, it is helpful to have a basic understanding of how computer programs work, even if you don't necessarily know how to write them yourself.

While they can do incredibly complex things, all computer programs essentially work by asking a series of yes or no questions. When we think about all "data" ultimately consisting of 1's and 0's, or binary code, what those 1's and 0's represent are "yes's" and "no's". Broadly speaking, there are no "maybes" for a computer. If we could write a simple computer program in English, it might look something like this:

Dear computer, if I am playing a video and I click the pause button, then please pause the video.

In this example, the computer will first need to check if I am playing a video. This is the first "yes or no" question it will need to answer. If the answer is "yes," I am playing a video, then it will ask question number two: am I clicking the pause button? Let's say I'm not. For as long as I am playing the video (i.e. as long as the first answer is still "yes"), the computer will wait, patiently, asking that second question over and over again until the answer is "yes." It's only mission in life, as long as I am playing a video, is to check constantly whether or not I am pressing the pause button. As soon as I do press the pause button, the answer to the second question becomes "yes," and then it will pause the video.

When we think about digital transactions happening with Bitcoin, what we're really doing when we participate in these transactions is executing a simple computer program. The essence of what happens is that Person A sends funds to Person B. Bitcoin's software will ask a series of questions: Does Person A actually have sufficient funding? Can Person A verify ownership of the address holding those funds? Is the address for Person B valid? As long as the correct inputs are provided, the decentralized Bitcoin network will reach a consensus for performing the computations and executing the program: the transaction will be verified and Person B will receive the funds.

With Bitcoin, the program that is running only deals with one type of transaction. "Bitcoins" are essentially just numbers that are moved around from one digital address to another, and the record of all of those moves is stored on the blockchain. The blockchain provides a system for a decentralized network of computers to reach a consensus about which tasks to perform and then to perform said tasks. In the case of Bitcoin, the "tasks" are transfers of coin from Person A to Person B, but is there any reason why this system couldn't be used to handle other types of tasks? Well, no, and that is precisely what Ethereum is built to do. Ethereum uses the same blockchain infrastructure, but it opens the door for any type of program to be executed.

Even when we continue to think in terms of financial transactions, the possibilities that Ethereum offers allow for things like conditions, creating a much more flexible environment for payment systems. For example, with Ethereum, a secure deposit could be held on the blockchain for a specified period of time: if a set of conditions were not met, it could be returned to the payer; if the conditions were met, the payment could be released to the payee. In Bitcoin, there is no way to hold a payment in "escrow" like this without the use of a third party. This kind of conditional transaction is a simple example of something that could be executed with a smart contract in Ethereum.

Another use case for smart contracts could include a 'multi-signature' approach to releases funds, meaning that a specified number of people must all agree to release the funds in order for the contract to be fulfilled. To further complicate matters, but also make them much more exciting, smart contracts are actually often used to trigger other smart contracts. For example, let's say you wanted to place a bet that your favorite sports team was going to win their next game: You could use one contract to place the bet, and in the background another smart contract would be used to gather data about the game and process the results, which would then send the outcome back to yet another smart contract to handle dispensing payout to the winner.

As we become more integrated into the Internet of Things, smart contracts open up a whole world of possibilities. For example, as smart cars become more prevalent, we could easily envision a transition from the old system of needing to put money in a parking meter to a system that would run entirely on smart contracts. Sensors could easily link specific cars to specific parking spaces, and a smart contract could be used to automatically deduct the appropriate fee based on the time a car was parked in a given space. Rather than digging around for change under the seat and dealing with parking meters, drivers could just park and the smart contract would manage the transaction in the background. Cities could do away with the entire system of meter maids and automate the entire process.

The concept of a supply chain can also serve as a good example for visualizing how smart contracts can be linked together in a real-world scenario. Let's say you go to a store and buy a toothbrush. This store normally only has 10 of these toothbrushes in stock, and you buy the last one. Many more are housed at a warehouse 100 miles away. They are manufactured, however, in China. The chemical plant that supplies the plastic to make this toothbrush is actually located in Texas.

At the point of exchange, when you buy the toothbrush, a network of smart contracts could immediately inform the warehouse that the store needs more inventory, which would, in turn, inform the manufacturer that they will need to get another shipment ready for the warehouse, which will, in turn, let the plastic supplier know that, in order to make more toothbrushes, the factory in China will need to have more raw materials shipped over to them.

The advantages to automating this entire system via smart contracts include eliminating a huge amount of paperwork, bureaucracy, delay time, human error, and fees associated with middlemen required in each instance to physically contact the next link up in the supply chain and negotiate each order. Making these incredibly complex systems more efficient and less vulnerable to corruption by creating a transparent record of every transaction is one of the most promising applications for smart contracts.

Despite the fundamental differences between Bitcoin and Ethereum, many people tend to treat these two projects as "competitors," battling for control of the blockchain space. Even for those who are only interested in Ether as a currency, and don't care particularly about the technology, this mindset is not really accurate. Ultimately, Bitcoin and Ethereum are two distinct, coexisting technologies that have different goals and applications. Bitcoin is designed to be a currency: it is an end in and of itself. Ethereum utilizes Ether as a way to execute smart contracts: the Ether currency is a means to end. In this sense, the two projects are not really competitors, in that, they both have different visions, goals, and uses.

In order to further grasp the concept of smart contracts, and how the Ethereum platform works, it is useful to explore some of the fundamentals of software development. If you have some experience working with any programming language, you will have an advantage in terms of understanding the way that code is executed using smart contracts. If not, don't worry. Again, you don't actually need to know how to write code in order to understand how Ethereum works, but it is useful to become familiar with some basic programming concepts.

Understanding the Concept of "State" in Applications

Within software development, there is a concept known as "state." Very basically, state refers to what is happening within an application at any given moment in time. Whenever something changes, that application's state changes.

For example, imagine you are visiting a web page that requires you to sign up for an account. You would most likely need to fill in a form with some information and click a "Submit" button to send your form to the website's server. You would then be taken to a "Welcome" page and given access to rest of the website. Behind the scenes, when you send in the form and the website takes you to the Welcome page, the state of the program being executed on the website changes.

Why does this matter? Smart contracts in Ethereum are ultimately programs or applications. Each iteration of an application's state is stored on the blockchain. This might sound complicated- and it is, in fact, pretty complicated- but this record of a program's history is fundamental to how smart contracts work in Ethereum. Within Ethereum applications, when a "transaction" occurs, software code can be triggered and executed. Thus, the state of that application can be changed and a record of what happened within the code is stored on the blockchain. By maintaining this record, the entire history of any given application's execution can be accessed and used to verify claims and regulate transactions.

Chapter 5: The Ethereum Virtual Machine (EVM)

All of the machines participating in the Ethereum network are called "nodes." Much like Bitcoin and other decentralized peer-to-peer networks, there are many nodes spread out all across the world. Anybody can choose to run a node. In terms of Ethereum, we can think of all of these different computers merging together, in a sense, to form one giant computer capable of performing distributed computations. This concept is known as the "Ethereum Virtual Machine," often abbreviated to EVM.

Virtual machines (or VM's), in computing terms, are emulated computer systems. If you've ever partitioned your hard-drive to run both Windows and OSX, you've used one kind of virtual machine. For our purposes, we don't really need to know too much about the role of virtual machines, in general. When it comes to the Ethereum Virtual Machine, the thing that is important to know is that it is the runtime environment for smart contracts. Each node on the Ethereum network runs an implementation of the EVM.

Like most virtual machines, the Ethereum Virtual Machine works at a very low-level, meaning that it processes code written in a "low-level" programming language. For developers, writing smart contracts is a lot more efficient when done in a "high-level" language. So, smart contracts are written in one language, usually Solidity, and then compiled (using a special program called a "compiler") into the low-level code that can be processed by the EVM environment.

Smart contracts run on the Ethereum Virtual Machine, which runs on each participating node. When we consider what we know about blockchain technology and what we have just covered concerning Ethereum, a few questions may arise.

First, if every instance of an application's state is stored on the blockchain, doesn't that mean the blockchain will become really, really big? Won't that make it difficult for nodes to continuously maintain it? How can smaller nodes use the network efficiently if they don't have the capacity to store the entire state? Good question!

If the Ethereum blockchain used the same approach and structure as Bitcoin- that is, if it simply recorded a long list of every single thing ever that happened with every application- it would indeed create problems in terms of efficiency and scalability. As you may have guessed, this is not exactly how it works.

In fact, this is one of the facets of the Ethereum blockchain that makes it unique, diverging from the architecture of the original blockchain as implemented by Bitcoin. Ethereum uses a particular kind of data structure based on a mathematical principle called a Merkle Tree. Bitcoin's blockchain also uses a Merkle Tree, but to get technical, Ethereum actually uses a special kind of Merkle Tree known as a Merkle Patricia Tree.

The Merkle Patricia Tree used by Ethereum is a way of storing data (i.e. the data that makes up the "blocks") as a set of key/value pairs. A "key" is a short code that corresponds to a specific "value," which can be a much longer piece of data.

These keys and values are generated and authenticated using cryptographically secure algorithms. Keys and values can only be generated in one very specific way using a particular mathematical method that only works in one direction. What this means is that any data (the value) that is fed into the algorithm will result in the same key every time. However, you cannot reverse the process by feeding a key into the system to arrive at the initial value.

Given the same set of keys and values, you would get the exact same Merkle Tree structure each and every time. Even a slight change in one bit of input data will yield a completely different output. Conceptually, this is the most important detail to grasp in terms of how verification works: any data that you feed into the algorithm will generate the identical cryptographically secure output each time as long as the data remains unchanged.

Thus far, what we have described is pretty much the same aspect of Merkle Trees that are used in the Bitcoin blockchain. What makes Ethereum's model different is the "Patricia" part of the Merkle Patricia Tree. This has to do with how the keys are positioned throughout the blockchains data structure.

Getting into the mathematical logic behind the scenes is a bit beyond the scope of this book, but broadly speaking the system is able to decide how to merge and arrange data stored in blocks by using prefixes that are assigned to each key. What this means, practically speaking, is that nodes have the ability to verify authenticity without needing to download the entire blockchain.

In fact, individual nodes will almost never need to access the entire state of the system to perform a given computation. Downloading the entire blockchain, therefore, would not be very efficient. Instead, a node can download only the partial state that it needs, and it can verify that chunk of code (or that "branch of the tree") by checking it, using the keys, against the surrounding branches. Because the surrounding branches will contain a reference linked all the way back to the root (the very first transaction), nodes can verify the partial state without needing to download the entire state history. This makes transactions in Ethereum much faster, more efficient, and allows for greater scalability of the platform.

Chapter 6: The Role of Ether in Smart Contracts

Smart contracts, we have learned, are computer programs, or "scripts," written in code. These scripts are written in a Turing-complete programming language. "Turing-complete," by definition, means that this language is capable of doing any kind of computation. If something can be expressed with an algorithm, a Turing-complete language can express it. While there are a few languages that can be used to write smart contracts, the most popular today is called Solidity. Solidity is similar in many ways to JavaScript, a very versatile and widely used programming language notable for its use in web applications.

One major problem posited by Turing-complete machines (i.e. any machine capable of running scripts written in a Turing-complete language) is known as the "halting problem." Basically, what this means is that the computer has no way of knowing in advance whether a program will stop at some point, or if it will loop forever and ever and ever (in programming terms, this is known as an "infinite loop"). The only way to determine this is by actually running the code.

For example, imagine I had a program that said something like: "Dear computer, please give me a random number." While it is possible that I could get a number like 50 or 300, you might also notice that I did not specify a length. It is entirely possible that the computer would spit out a number so long that, if unchecked, it could go on and on and on towards infinity. A better idea might be to tell the computer, "Dear computer, please give me a random number less than 1000." Then, of course, it could spit out a negative number that headed on towards infinity. So, I might tell it, "Ok, fine, please give me a random number between 0 and 1000." The poor computer is just trying to do its job, but this time it might spit out a number like 1.500000... followed by infinite o's. Really, to get our program to work, we would need to specify that we want a whole number, or integer, between 0 and 1000.

Getting programs to run the way we want them to is not always easy, and it is not uncommon for programming bugs to lead inadvertently to "infinite loops." A machine has no way of knowing whether or not it will run into an infinite loop in a piece of code until it actually runs that code, at which point it is stuck. If any node on the Ethereum network got stuck running a program in an infinite loop, it would effectively halt the entire system, hence being called "the halting problem." This inability to complete a script would stop new data from being added to the blockchain. That would, obviously, be bad. So, how can we avoid this problem?

The answer is actually pretty simple: Ether. Within the Ethereum network, computation is not free. Every time a user makes a request to run a script, a certain fee is associated, which is paid in Ether. Furthermore, in order to run a script, a user must set a limit to the amount of Ether put towards running that script. The Ether dedicated to running a particular script is known as "gas." If the script runs out of Ether, or "gas", before completion, it will simply halt at its current state.

By requiring a fee and forcing a value cap to be set for each script, Ethereum eliminates the problem of infinitely looping programs, be they accidental, or, as is more likely the case, malicious denial-of-service attacks. Nobody has an infinite amount of Ether, so even if a bad actor attempted to execute an infinitely looping program they would not be able to sustain the funding required to continue running the program. The script would be cut off from executing as soon as the funding ran out.

Ether, as a currency, plays an integral role in the Ethereum framework. Outside of usage as "gas" towards executing smart contracts on the Ethereum blockchain, however, Ether is also traded on many popular exchanges for other cryptocurrencies and some fiat currencies, like dollars and euros.

In the US you can buy Ether with fiat currency through several digital currency exchanges, including Coinbase, Bittrex, and others. You can buy Ether with Bitcoin through almost all notable exchanges, including ShapeShift, Kraken, Poloniex, and more. Depending on where you are in the world, your access to specific exchanges will vary, but you should have no trouble buying, selling, or trading Ether through one or more online platforms no matter where you live.

Ether has a significant real-world value beyond the role of "gas." One Ether has reached a value of over $300 at several periods throughout 2017. For many, Ether is treated exclusively as an investment, with speculators exchanging Bitcoin or other digital currencies for Ether in hopes that the value of Ether will increase. If it does, they may simply trade their Ether back into fiat without ever really engaging with any applications on the Ethereum network. In this sense, Ether can be bought, sold, and traded like Bitcoin or any other digital currency. Within the Ethereum framework, however, Ether serves a unique purpose as "gas" for running smart contracts.

Even if your interest in Ethereum is purely as a financial investment and you don't plan on writing software or being involved in any way with applications built on the platform, it is helpful to understand the relationship between those applications, the structure of the Ethereum ecosystem, and the value of Ether as a currency.

We know that Ether can be bought on various currency exchanges, but where does Ether actually come from? Who makes it and how? As of the time of this writing, Ether is "mined" in a manner similar to Bitcoin. Nodes in the Ethereum network perform complex math problems in order to validate transactions. When a particular node, or miner, successfully "solves a block," that block is added to the blockchain and the miner is rewarded for their work with a certain amount of Ether. This structure may be changing in the near future, however, and it leads us to another important concept.

We need to look a bit more closely at the role of mining, how transactions are validated, how the blockchain is maintained, and how this relates to the future of Ethereum.

Chapter 7: Consensus Algorithms: Proof-of-Work vs. Proof-of-Stake

A significant part of what drives the real-world implementation of blockchain protocols involves conducting secure transactions, whether they are purely financial transactions as with Bitcoin or whether they are transactions of other types of information or data. When one party sends information to another, how does the system guarantee that the information is valid?

We have touched already on the concept of a distributed ledger, and the role of decentralized networks in maintaining a blockchain. As a practical matter, what this means is that many people all over the world need to run software that validates transactions and records those transactions to the blockchain. In some cases, this can get quite expensive in terms of both computer power and electricity. To encourage people to participate, we can imagine that they might need some incentive. This is where "mining" comes in.

Bitcoin miners notoriously require specialized equipment that performs thousands of complex mathematical operations every second. These calculations eat up significant processing power and consume a lot of electricity. We will not go too in-depth into how Bitcoin mining works, specifically, but the general idea is that miners compete to solve a complex math problem in order to validate each new block that is added to the blockchain.

The solution to the problem, each time, is basically a random number, and the only way to find it is by trial and error. So, miners use their equipment to try out tons of random numbers as quickly as possible until they find one that matches the criteria set forth by the core code of the Bitcoin software. When a miner thinks they have found a solution, they broadcast this to the entire Bitcoin network and other miners check their solution. When a majority of miners agrees that the solution is correct, the block is added to the blockchain and the miner who found the solution is rewarded with brand new Bitcoin that are generated from the Bitcoin software. For active miners, the potential for earning the reward outweighs the cost incurred by running mining equipment, which encourages participation in the system.

This model is known as "Proof-of-Work." Because the only way to solve the problem required to validate a block is via trial and error, there is no way for a miner produce a correct result and get the reward other than by doing the work of computation.

Like Bitcoin, Ethereum has historically worked on a "Proof-of-Work" consensus model. However, in early 2017 it was announced that Ethereum intends to shift towards implementing a "Proof-of-Stake" consensus model in the near future. Vitalik Buterin, Ethereum's creator, released a whitepaper in May of 2017 proposing the implementation of a new Proof-of-Stake algorithm called Casper into the Ethereum protocol. The timeframe remains unclear, but early reports suggest that the Casper algorithm will be phased in over time. Ethereum enthusiasts have met this news with mixed feelings, and there is ongoing speculation as to how Proof-of-Stake will translate into real-world applications.

In order to understand how this might impact Ethereum, let's explore how Proof-of-Stake generally works. When looking at Proof-of-Work, we saw that there is a real-world cost associated with performing what are essentially meaningless calculations in order to find a random number to solve a block and claim a reward. To get a sense of how significant this cost is, it is estimated that both Bitcoin and Ethereum eat up over $1 million per day in electricity and hardware costs associated with mining.

Ethereum's proposed Proof-of-Stake (PoS) model eliminates the resource drain presented by PoW. Rather than relying on miners, participants in this model take on the role of "validators." Similar to placing a bet, validators stake a certain amount of their own Ether towards solving a block. The higher the amount a validator stakes, the greater the probability that they will solve the block. If they "win," they will be rewarded.

In the event that a bad actor attempts to manipulate the system, their stake will simply disappear out of circulation. The Ether they have put towards attempting to validate a false transaction, for example, will be eliminated from the total amount of Ether in existence. In theory, this will increase the overall value of the currency due to the principle of scarcity. In economics, the scarcity principle basically implies that where there is demand, the less of commodity there is, the greater its value.

The Casper algorithm represents a new model for implementing Proof-of-Stake consensus in a real-world environment. Among Ethereum users and throughout the larger cryptocurrency and blockchain community, there is much ongoing debate over PoW versus PoS, both generally and in relation to Ethereum, specifically.

If successful, some of the advantages of Proof-of-Stake include the aforementioned elimination of resource consumption required for mining, and potentially a greater level of security and scalability. Faster transactions speeds may also be a result. However, until the Casper algorithm is implemented, many of these possibilities remain theoretical, and many skeptics maintain the attitude of, "I'll believe it when I see it."

As a platform for handling smart contracts, Ethereum opens up the potential of blockchain technology for a wide variety of applications by creating a secure, hack-proof, trustless environment for creating and executing smart contracts. Fundamental to this platform is the way in which transactions of information are validated, and validation is handled by the consensus algorithm. Consensus algorithms are a big deal in terms of the functionality of a decentralized blockchain environment. Naturally, there are those who are apprehensive and have concerns about how shifting the consensus algorithm from Proof-of-Work to Proof-of-Stake may impact Ethereum. Some, of course, believe that Proof-of-Stake will present a positive evolution in terms of improving the efficiency of the blockchain architecture.

Will Proof-of-Stake actually perform as intended when implemented in the real world? The answer remains to be seen, but for those with a vested interest in Ethereum, this is an important space to watch moving forward.

Chapter 8: Ethereum (ETH) vs. Ethereum Classic (ETC)

For those who are in the early stages of discovering the cryptocurrency space, one hurdle that may catch the eye is the existence of Ethereum Classic, abbreviated as ETC on many popular exchanges and cryptocurrency tickers. What is the difference between Ethereum and Ethereum Classic?

If you aren't confused enough already, in order to

understand Ethereum Classic it is necessary, also, to become familiar with The DAO. DAO, in general, stands for "decentralized autonomous organization." The DAO was a specific decentralized autonomous organization that was launched on the Ethereum blockchain in 2016. The DAO was designed to offer a model for a new kind of institutional structure, useful for both businesses and non-profit organizations. This particular venture issued a token sale in May of 2016 as a way to crowd-fund development. This token sale was very successful and raised around $150-million in under a month. Then, The DAO's code was hacked just one month later, in June of 2016. Hackers used a known vulnerability in the code to reallocate around one-third of the money into a different account, valued at around $50 million at the time of the attack.

In July of 2016, after the hack, there was a decision within the Ethereum community to "hard-fork" the blockchain. A "fork" in a blockchain is much like a fork in a road- a split, where one path becomes two. In the case of Ethereum, hard-forking the blockchain made it possible to go back and recover the stolen funds and return them to The DAO.

The DAO hard-fork created a large dispute within the Ethereum community. A significant number of participants in the network were against splitting the blockchain, and as a result, they continued to maintain the pre-forked chain. The pre-forked version of the blockchain became Ethereum Classic. The other members of the Ethereum network moved over to the new blockchain, which continued on as Ethereum. Since then, Ethereum has forked a few more times in response to other attacks, strengthening its defenses against DDoS attacks and spamming in the meantime. The subsequent forks were not nearly as controversial and did not spawn "competing versions" of Ethereum.

There continues to be an ongoing debate within the Ethereum community over the role of Ethereum Classic and the larger politics surrounding blockchain forks. There are some who are ideologically opposed to the idea of forking, no matter what, arguing that the inherent value and guiding principle of a blockchain are that it cannot be altered. Others believe that forking can be a necessary, acceptable, and useful way for blockchain projects to adapt in response to changing circumstances, technological advances, and user demands.

Debate exists concerning investment viability as well as ideology. There are those who will assert that Ethereum Classic is "dead," and those who believe it will ultimately overtake Ethereum as the dominant "fork" of the blockchain, the latter of which are a minority. Looking at the history of both in terms of their respective currencies, it is safe to say that the majority of investors seem to trend, thus far, towards Ethereum rather than Ethereum Classic.

Chapter 9: Decentralized Applications (dApps) Built On The Ethereum Platform

We've talked about Ethereum as a platform for building decentralized applications (dApps), but we haven't really explored what these look like in much depth. Bearing in mind, once again, that this technology has only existed for a few years, we have already seen a number of very interesting projects emerge that are built on top of the Ethereum architecture.

The focus of this book is primarily on Ethereum, itself, but it is worth looking at some of the ways this platform has been implemented in different applications and real-world scenarios.

One of the core features of Ethereum is that it allows anyone to issue their own digital token or currency. Ether is used as "gas" to finance the execution of smart contracts within the Ethereum ecosystem. Applications built on top of Ethereum's code base, but suited towards performing a specific function, may choose to create their own token to use as "gas" within their particular blockchain ecosystem.

One example to illustrate this concept is the Golem project. Golem is one of the most well-established and widely known applications build on the Ethereum framework, and it has its own currency, also called Golem (GNT).

The general idea behind Golem is to create a platform for decentralized computing. Lots of people have computers. Most people don't really use their computers to their full capacity all of the time, if ever. This means that many people have access to a lot of unused computer power. Golem's vision is to create a system for people to securely "rent" their unused computer power to people who need it to perform high-level computations. Things like rendering graphics, for example, take a lot of computer power- the more complex the job, the more expensive it becomes, eventually requiring access to resources that can be prohibitive in many situations.

Instead of needing to go to a fancy studio to render a complex set of graphics, or having to access a professional infrastructure to process a large amount of data, Golem's goal is to create on-demand access to large amounts of computer power through a distributed network- with lots of participants contributing resources to one task. Transactions happen using smart contracts and payment happens in the Golem token. Ethereum's secure blockchain infrastructure opens the door to projects like this to develop.

Another example of a project using the Ethereum backbone is BAT or Basic Attention Token. This is a new platform for digital advertising under development by the creator of JavaScript and the co-founder of Mozilla. BAT uses its own privacy-focused web browser to track user attention anonymously, keeping private information secure and sending anonymous information back to advertisers. Users can choose to opt-in and be shown targeted ads, and they will be rewarded with BAT for their attention. Advertisers, in turn, are rewarded with BAT based on how much engagement their ads receive. By managing all of this information on a secure blockchain, the creators of BAT suggest that the capacity for fraudulent or malicious advertising is greatly reduced, the privacy of consumers is protected, and the efficiency of ad targeting is greatly improved.

Golem and BAT are two examples of very different projects utilizing their own tokens, both of which are built on the Ethereum framework. Of course, there are many more "dApps" out there, and undoubtedly many more that will be developed in the near future as Ethereum continues to gain traction and break into the mainstream.

The possibilities for deploying smart contracts on the blockchain are virtually limitless, particularly as the infrastructure for implementing blockchain-based systems develops. For example, let's pretend you owned an amusement park. For years, you've been selling tickets that can be used for various rides, games, and snacks. People buy a certain number of tickets at a kiosk before they enter the park, and then they use tickets for everything inside.

Instead of selling tickets, you could create your own token through Ethereum. Customers could download an app, buy tokens, and access rides automatically. If someone was out of tokens, they couldn't access the ride without buying more, which they could do easily from the app. With a secure blockchain system, nobody could claim to lose tickets, have tickets stolen, or sneak onto rides.

The amusement park example may be a bit silly, but the same concept could be applied to many more serious contexts. For example, the government in Dubai is making use of Ethereum in its stated goal of becoming the first blockchain-powered government by the year 2020. Dubai has estimated, thus far, that it can save $1.5 billion dollars simply by optimizing document processing through implementing a blockchain system.

Many other governments, including Japan, China, and the US have expressed interest in exploring blockchain technology to streamline government services. In Ukraine, a startup company using the Ethereum platform was contracted in 2017 to pilot test a new property management system.

The blockchain revolution is undoubtedly underway, and Ethereum is a major player, leading the way in many sectors. From an investment perspective, many people see a lot of potential in Ethereum and decentralized blockchain applications. Before deciding whether to invest in Ethereum or an Ethereum-based project, it is a good idea to explore some of the potential downsides in addition to the promising elements.

Chapter 10: The Ethereum Enterprise Alliance (EEA)

Given the surge of enthusiasm directed towards blockchain and cryptocurrencies in 2017, it should come as no surprise that a number of Fortune 500 companies have begun to explore these technologies. In March of 2017, a non-profit organization called The Ethereum Enterprise Alliance (EEA) was launched. The EEA is comprised of a variety of start-ups, think tanks, Fortune 500 companies, and others working with the Ethereum framework.

The vision of the EEA is focused primarily on the development of "private" Ethereum-based blockchains designed for enterprise environments. Unlike public blockchains, so-called "private" blockchains would not be visible or accessible to anyone. These in-house blockchains would require permission to access. Many within the larger blockchain community see this move as counterintuitive, as much of the appeal of blockchain architecture is related precisely to the fact that it is decentralized, open, and eliminates the need for trust in a third party. Skeptics have raised the question of how "private blockchains" will differ, fundamentally, from intranets. This remains to be seen.

That being said, the EEA has gained a huge amount of support throughout the early months of its existence. Many big-name members are investing substantially in the development of "private blockchains," including companies like IBM, JP Morgan, Microsoft, Intel, and Deloitte. How will corporate adoption of blockchain technology impact the vision of open, decentralized, peer-to-peer exchanges? This is one question that looms large in the minds of many independent investors and those who see the possibilities for blockchain technology to create systemic change and re-imagine institutional structures.

Chapter 11: Criticisms, Risks, & Challenges Concerning Ethereum

Any new technology faces obstacles and challenges as it moves into the real world, and Ethereum is no exception. While there is enthusiastic support, an active community and obvious potential surrounding Ethereum, anybody who wants to get involved should also be aware that challenges and risks exist, as well.

Because the Ethereum platform is open and accessible, many companies and projects have sprung up around the Ethereum ecosystem, building projects on the Ethereum blockchain. In the long run, this is probably a good thing. When we consider the big picture and remember that we are still in the early stages of exploring this technology, a diverse group of initial developers competing to create decentralized applications will, in theory, ultimately strengthen the Ethereum platform.

In the short term, however, this climate has led to a huge surge in "ICO's," or Initial Coin Offerings. ICO's are a largely unregulated way for companies to raise capital for a new cryptocurrency-based project. A form of crowd-funding, ICO's typically sell a percentage of a new cryptocurrency or token to a group of early investors in exchange for some other form of legal tender, usually Bitcoin. This method of fundraising gives startups a way to bypass many of the stringent regulations involved in raising venture capital or borrowing from banks through the traditional means. This is very similar to IPO's selling shares of a company to raise money for future plans or operations, except in this case rather than buying stock an investor would buy virtual currency.

For investors, buying in early to a promising project can have a lot of appeal. If the project is successful, the value of the associated currency will increase, thus potentially giving them a sizeable profit. Because ICO's are unregulated by financial authorities like the SEC (Securities Exchange Commission), however, there is a risk of fraudulent ICO scams.

While ICO's can be very successful and lucrative ventures, this can be a high-risk space. Particularly considering that anyone can issue their own currency fairly easily with Ethereum, it is important to perform due diligence as an investor. You can't swing a cat in cyberspace without hitting an ICO developing a new Ethereum-based application that promises to make early investors into millionaires.

Beyond the potential for fraud, there are some other potential concerns that come with the ICO model as it relates to Ethereum. In many cases, early investors in a promising project are actually companies rather than private individuals. One result of the ICO model in the Ethereum space is that we end up with companies holding a lot of Ether, rather than individuals, per se. In terms of Ether as a currency, it is important to consider the implications of having large amounts of Ether tied up in companies.

Simply put, companies have expenses. They need to pay employees, pay for office space, marketing, etc. What if one big company has a successful funding round, gains a lot of Ether from investors, and then doesn't really develop anything that great? That company still needs to pay its expenses. Perhaps they dump all of their Ether at once and cash out. Sizeable "dumps" like this affect the price of any currency, and if one big company dumps, others may see the price drop, become alarmed, and begin to dump their holdings as well, thus snowballing into a huge price drop that ultimately screws individual investors the most.

This is not necessarily an inevitable scenario, and it is certainly not a potential problem that is exclusive to Ethereum, but it is one concern that arises when a handful of large companies hold a considerable amount of Ether.

As a potential investor, it is always a good idea to do your own research. Read white papers, engage in discussions, and determine for yourself whether or not you think a project is solid. Marketing and hype can play a big role in this space, and following the crowd into the ICO flavor-of-the-month is often far more likely to end up in a loss than a profit.

One of the biggest concerns from voices within the broader Ethereum community is the way that third-party applications may impact the underlying Ethereum platform. This applies to the potential for fraudulent ICO's to issue a scam currency using Ethereum's infrastructure, but it can also apply to well-intentioned efforts.

We know that Ethereum is a platform for building decentralized applications. We know, also, that part of the appeal of the Ethereum platform is the capacity to execute applications on a blockchain. The potential for this vision is very exciting, but baked into the reality of actually building dApps on the Ethereum platform is the fact that writing software is hard.

Finding developers who can write good, bug-free software for Android or iOS can be difficult even though those are hugely popular platforms upon which many applications are built. When it comes to developing applications for the Ethereum blockchain, finding developers who can write code in the Solidity language, or other languages being used to implement smart contracts, can be even more challenging. In fact, many very good programmers today have never even heard of Ethereum!

As the demand for developers who can write code in the Solidity language continues to grow, there is an opportunity for aspiring programmers to find work in this field and comparatively little competition. While there are definitely some talented programmers working with Ethereum, it is important to remember that "smart contracts" have only existed for a few years, and therefore even talented programmers may have relatively little experience with this type of software development.

Naturally, any new technology will go through a similar process in its early days. When considering Ethereum, however, it is important to think about the impact that potential vulnerabilities in applications built on the Ethereum blockchain might have on Ether as a currency. If one or more applications built on the Ethereum platform suffers from a significant hack or is full of bugs, how will that affect the value of Ether?

It is impossible to predict the future, but for a potential investor, it is a good idea to think seriously about how third-party applications built on the Ethereum platform might impact the perception of the platform itself, and subsequently the value of Ether. Of course, large-scale adoption and a series of successful dApps running on Ethereum could impact the value of Ether in a positive way, and that is clearly the direction in which serious investors believe the project to be heading. (Otherwise, one can assume, they would not be serious investors).

Chapter 12: Getting Started with Ethereum

If you feel as though you would like to learn about the nuts and bolts of Ethereum, or are thinking of hiring someone to create an Ethereum based application, then exploring this chapter will be beneficial.

If not, we suggest you skip this chapter and come back to it at a time you feel that it will become more relevant to you.

To start using the Ethereum platform one will need a specific piece of software – AKA a client – that is able to run contracts and network with other computers using specific protocols.

There are multiple clients written in different languages, which helps to broaden support for the network and gives choice to programmers with various strengths.

As with most projects, it helps to have multiple teams to implement the protocols at this tends to make them more reliable and robust – using cross-reference checks and various tried and tested checking methods.

There are several clients that run on top of the wallet, offering additional features, the more notable of which were compiled by CoinDesk and are outlined below:

- Ethereum (J). A Java version.

- EthereumH. A version was written in the Haskell programming language.

- Go-ethereum. Written in Google's Go language, this is currently the most popular ethereum client. Commonly called "geth", it includes a mining component while allowing users the ability to create contracts and transfer funds between addresses

- Parity. A low-footprint version written in a language called Rust, spawned by Mozilla.

- Pyethapp. A Python implementation that includes mining and virtual machine capabilities. This has been subcontracted to a team at Brainbot, led by Heiko Hees.

- Ruby-Ethereum. A version was written in the Ruby web application programming language.

- Cpp ethereum. Led by Christian Reitwiessner, cpp ethereum is a C++ client.

Ethereumjs-lib. An implementation in JavaScript

If you are not comfortable working in command line, there is a simple tutorial on http://ethereum.org/token that will help you create a token. There are also step-by-step instructions on how to implement a contract via that token.

Once you're more familiar, Christian Reitwiessner has elaborated on the developing social ethics and best practices of smart contract development in public presentations.

Learning Solidity

To begin with, having a solid basis in JavaScript will be extremely helpful in learning Solidity.

If you are not comfortable working in command line, there is a simple tutorial on:

http://ethereum.org/token

Whether you know JavaScript or not, here is a list of resources you can use to learn more about coding in Solidity:

Solidity Documentation – The most comprehensive resource for Solidity, this tutorial is geared toward people familiar with programming, but who may not have experience with ethereum or blockchain technology in general.

Ether.fund – This online resource maintains a list of example Solidity contracts that can be a useful resource for developing your own contracts or understanding how different methods of creating contracts work.

Ethereum Github Wiki – A community maintained a wiki for the technology, this resource contains a list of resources for dapp developers that will be most useful for those with some programming background. These include tools, code examples, development environments and technical references.

ConsenSys – If you are new to programming and the ethereum blockchain, you might find this "Intro to Programming Smart Contracts" by ethereum startup ConsenSys useful. It introduces basic concepts in dapp development and walks the reader through one possible dapp development workflow.

Ledger Labs – Another "Intro to Dapp Development" tutorial is available from Canada-based blockchain consultancy Ledger Labs. While a work in progress, it currently walks the reader through installing Geth, running a local node, a basic contract design and a more advanced auction contract example.

If you are completely new to programming, you might find that you need to first learn the basic concepts involved in any coding.

Online interactive platform Codeacademy has free interactive tutorials that will teach you the basics of JavaScript, the language on which Solidity is based. While the details and syntax are different, many of the basic concepts you will learn are still applicable in Solidity.

Chapter 13: The Future of Ethereum, Decentralized Applications & Blockchain Technology

The value of Ether reached record highs in 2017, and many speculate that the value will continue to trend upwards over time. Many major companies have adopted the Ethereum vision of a flexible blockchain platform with the ability to utilize smart contracts. As the promise of blockchain technology becomes clearer on a global scale, a surge of entrepreneurs has emerged seeking to integrate this technology into every field from energy to healthcare to politics.

Whether the Ethereum platform will ultimately become the definitive framework for building decentralized blockchain applications remains to be seen. It is possible that Ethereum is akin to an early web browser like NetScape Navigator and that some future effort will become the "Google of blockchain." Considering how new this technology is, it would be naïve not to consider that possibility. Of course, it is also conceivable that Ethereum will continue to grow, improve, and ultimately dominate this space. The upcoming update to using the Casper algorithm and the Proof-of-Stake model will serve as one test in terms of Ethereum's ability to evolve.

Whether you plan to invest in Ether, another token issued through an Ethereum-based application, or you are interested in building your own dApp on the Ethereum blockchain, it is important to stay informed. Technology changes in this space incredibly quickly, and as blockchain enters major industries, we will likely begin to see changes in terms of how cryptocurrencies and blockchain applications are regulated. Joining online communities and conversations, such as Reddit, Slack channels, and via Twitter are a great way to stay current on developments in the Ethereum platform. Learning about other platforms, reading whitepapers, and becoming familiar with the leading thinkers in this field is a good way to develop a deeper understanding and broader perspective, which can help you formulate your own opinions about what technologies are likely to succeed and how to invest and participate.

How the future will play out is, of course, something that we cannot foresee. Whatever the future looks like, however, it is almost certainly going to be shaped by blockchain technology. Today, Ethereum offers one of the most well-established and innovative approaches to making this technology accessible, flexible, and exciting. For investors, developers, and entrepreneurs in this cutting-edge space, the possibilities are unlimited.

Lightning Source UK Ltd.
Milton Keynes UK
UKHW021141120821
388748UK00011B/726

9 781803 607801